MW00332748

Policing Muslim Communities

Farrukh B. Hakeem · M.R. Haberfeld
Arvind Verma

Policing Muslim Communities

Comparative International Context

 Springer

Farrukh B. Hakeem
Social Sciences
Shaw University
Raleigh, NC, USA

M.R. Haberfeld
John Jay College of Criminal Justice
City University of New York
New York, NY, USA

Arvind Verma
Department of Criminal Justice
Indiana University
Bloomington, IN, USA

ISBN 978-1-4614-3551-8   ISBN 978-1-4614-3552-5 (eBook)
DOI 10.1007/978-1-4614-3552-5
Springer New York Heidelberg Dordrecht London

Library of Congress Control Number: 2012935519

Printed on acid-free paper

Springer is part of Springer Science+Business Media (www.springer.com)

This was a very challenging but rewarding intellectual endeavor and though it took a lot of time, energy, and effort the end product was very satisfying and it was well worth the effort. I would like to dedicate this effort to my family (wife, Shuby, and children, Farha and Shagufta) who were forced to sacrifice a lot due to my intellectual preoccupations. I would also like to acknowledge and thank my Indian friends, Jay Rathore, (actually His Highness Prince Puranjay Sinh), the owner of the Raghubir Sinh Library, Sitamau, India (now called Sri Natnagar Shodh Samsthan) and his able secretary/manager Manohar Singh Ranawat, for generously hosting me at their library and letting me collect research materials from the priceless and rare works in their private collections.

Farrukh B. Hakeem

As already evident from my previous work, this volume is again a product of my upbringing in three countries located on three different continents and the lessons and torments to which this life experience exposed me. I dedicate this work to my mother, Dr. Lucja Sadykiewicz who, when I was a child growing up in Poland, asked me to promise her that once we emigrate to Israel I will befriend an Arab girl, and to my daughters, Nellie and Mia, who always accept people the way they are without any prejudice or bias.

M.R. Haberfeld

Scholarly work is always an arduous task and especially demanding upon family members. Such writings entail long hours of separation, excuse from daily chores, and patience from loved ones. I dedicate this work to my wife, Chapla, and children, Juhi and Rishi, whose support made this work possible.

Arvind Verma

Preface

The idea for this book was initiated when the three of us decided that there was a paucity of empirically validated literature regarding the policing of Muslim societies. This was an area that was rife with various myths, stereotypes, and prejudices masquerading as received science and had not been studied from a social scientific perspective. The present work is an initial attempt to remedy this deficiency. The authors attempt to distinguish between two different approaches to policing. The first is the current approach to police administration by government agencies, and secondly, an ideal alternative approach, which applies the findings of evidence-based research for the benefit of local communities, and the society at large.

With the advent of the twenty-first century, law enforcement agencies have taken on an important dimension in international criminal justice. Globally, scholars of policing have witnessed a shift in focus from the traditionally reactive, law-and-order and crime control model of policing to one that is more just and equitable and is accountable to the community so as to ensure support. Using evidence-based research and applying theories that make police more accountable and democratic are some of the best safeguards towards achieving lasting gains in public order, and also making improvements towards the protection of human rights. With the emergence of the new globalized social structures, traditional boundaries and threats have now taken on new forms. There is a need to balance the public safety concerns of society with those of human rights violations. This transition from law-and-order policing, to a problem-oriented policing model calls for more systemic and structural changes in modern police forces. In order to garner the support of local communities police agencies need to find ways not to be perceived as an undemocratic occupying force, set up to harass and intimidate marginalized communities; one such way may possibly be a change in the composition of the force that will mirror more closely the population it polices.

Police forces today face challenges in finding effective methods to mobilize diverse communities and garner their support in combating terrorism and international crime control. A failure to get cooperation from all sections of the community challenges the legitimacy of the policing endeavor and makes their task less effective. This work is an exploratory study that examines the issue of policing Muslim societies, using evidence-based research and the application of accumulated knowledge regarding the policing of religious minorities. At a later stage, attempts will be made to commence research in this field by surveying the communities, initially starting with focus group interviews. This process should build on the current science of policing and should offer scholars with more insight into a much neglected area of policing.

Raleigh, NC   Farrukh B. Hakeem
New York, NY   M.R. Haberfeld
Bloomington, IN   Arvind Verma

Contents

Chapter 1
Introduction: Policing by Religion

When the authors of this volume got together to conceptualize the themes of *Policing Muslim Communities*, the idea that the largest police force in the United States, the New York City Police department, the famous NYPD, will contemplate an operational concept referred to as Human Terrain Mapping, the "Muslim Initiative" or the "Moroccan Initiative," seemed truly unthinkable if not reprehensive (Associate Press 2011; Deepa 2012; Cincotta 2012; Patel & Goitein 2012; Religious Profiling).

Yet, in 2011, the Associated Press unveiled details of such an initiative to the unsuspecting audience or maybe the audience was indeed not so unsuspecting. It is possible that in the aftermath of September 11th, 2001 attacks on the United States, the general public became socialized to the idea that certain segments of society should be policed in a specific manner, or "policing by religion" became an acceptable and legitimate tactic to be used by local law enforcement.

Despite a certain degree of denial that accompanied the publicity around the Muslim Initiative, overall the time allocated to the discussion around this, seemingly very disturbing concept, was rather minimal. It is possible that the public, who responded in a rather catatonic manner to the various disturbing aspects of the Patriot Act (ACLU 2012), is already desensitized to the very dangerous labels that have been applied to the basic freedoms any democracy promised and supposedly affords its citizens, and more specifically to practice their religion free from persecution and fear.

Although the initial goal of this volume was based on a personal discussion with colleagues to examine issues of policing in Muslim societies, it quickly evolved into a much larger concept of tackling the issues of human rights in a rapidly changing political landscape that demands a different and more sensitive type of law enforcement. This book seeks to examine policing via the following method: policing in Muslim majority countries (Sunni/Shia), a country where Muslims are a minority, a Western country, a non-Western country, and countries where Muslims are under military control.

F.B. Hakeem et al., *Policing Muslim Communities: Comparative International Context*, DOI 10.1007/978-1-4614-3552-5_1, © Springer Science+Business Media New York 2012

It seeks to examine the local response to policing in these countries and elicit reactions of the local communities to the administration of policing by the local authorities. The authors endeavor to distinguish between two different approaches: the current approach to police administration as administered by government agencies, and an alternative approach that would be considered as an ideal by the local community.

With the advent of the twenty-first century law enforcement agencies have taken on an important dimension in international criminal justice. Practitioners and scholars of policing around the globe have witnessed a shift in focus from the traditionally reactive law-and-order and crime control stance to the demands for accountability so as to ensure the support of the community in reducing crime and disorder. Making the police more accountable and democratizing the police forces is one of the best safeguards towards achieving lasting gains in public order and also making improvements towards protection of human rights.

Though human rights concerns are important these need to be balanced with public safety concerns of societies. In an increasingly globalized world, a new infrastructure has emerged along with new coalitions. The traditional boundaries and threats have become more diffused. Threats by groups in a society can coalesce and materialize much faster and, if unresolved, can become problematic when police forces do not adapt accordingly. With the shift of the policing endeavor from its traditional task of controlling local disorder it will be faced with meeting new challenges. With the transformation of police forces now mirroring practices that are akin to those who are on the front lines in the war on terror, the danger of sliding into a military ethos for police forces could lead to a challenge of its legitimacy and will render them less effective.

Police forces face challenges in finding effective methods to mobilize diverse communities and garner their support and assistance in combating terrorism and international crime control. This volume is an exploratory study of policing Muslim societies and its unique feature is the overview of policing of Muslim communities in different geopolitical environments that differ from each other in the most extreme manner yet happen to display certain law enforcement commonalities.

In the present political context this book is sorely needed given that many Muslim countries around the globe have been faced with a crisis in governance. Consequently, what is an essentially police problem of order maintenance has deteriorated to such an extent that many of these countries are now under military occupation or control. Afghanistan, Yemen, Iraq, Somalia, and Pakistan are some of the examples of this phenomenon and this list may grow in the future.

The thrust of the book is to examine policing from three main perspectives: policing by Muslims, policing with Muslims, and policing of Muslims. Chapter 2, the "Concept of Punishment Under Sharia," discusses the origin of the Sharia as a unique legal system when compared to other legal systems. It is based primarily on the Quran, which was revealed to Prophet Muhammad more than 1,400 years ago, and is considered to be an all-encompassing system that expresses the Divine will. Theories of Islamic law developed during the second century of the Islamic calendar (about 800 CE). Later schools of thought developed with each school based on the writings of scholars (*fuqaha*) dealing with different aspects of law, based on their varying interpretations of the Quran and the Hadith. Muslims believe that the renewal of society requires a return to Islam, which draws inspiration from the two main sources, Quran and Hadith. Ethical standards and legal rules govern not merely what humans are legally entitled to do, but also what they ought, in conscience, to do, or refrain from doing. As opposed to other legal systems, the Shariah is a comprehensive code that regulates conduct encompassing both the public and private domains by controlling the inner conscience and external social relations. This chapter scrutinizes the religious, social, and philosophical bases of crime and punishment under Islamic law. Each of the three kinds of punishments (Hadd, Taazir, and Qisas) are examined and the views of the various jurists from the different schools are analyzed. This enquiry also delves into the goals and policies that underlie this system of law and sets the framework for understanding of Muslim communities' views and attitudes towards law enforcement bodies.

Chapter 3, "Policing Muslims in Western Democracies," highlights the aftermaths of the incidents of September 9, 2011, when the Muslim community in the United States and in most western democracies has come under official and public scrutiny. Muslims, due to their particular culture, adherence to religious practices, and minority status have encountered hostility and even physical attacks. Their allegiance to countries of residence and to liberal democratic values has been questioned. Above all, the policing of Muslim communities in liberal societies have been a subject of increasing interest. There have been growing allegations of profiling and targeting of the Muslim youth by the security agencies. Intrusive surveillance, humiliating searches at the airports, and questionable stops on the roads have been reported by Muslims. On the other hand, security agencies have attempted to work with the community and hired minority officers to build bridges. This chapter examines the experiences of Muslim groups and the successes and failures of policing of their community in some selected western democracies.

Chapter 4, "Human Rights and Islamic Law," looks at the concept of power and its management in society. It examines the distribution and management of power, and the systems to correct the abuse of power in Muslim societies. After an examination of the International Bill of Human Rights, some of the mechanisms for incorporation of human rights through the doctrine of maslahah are examined. The doctrine of maslahah furnishes a balance between the highly idealistic levels of expectation from the government by the public and the efforts of the public to identify more meaningfully with Islam. The main premise of the chapter is the assertion that Human Rights and Islam are not incompatible.

Chapter 5, "Police and the Administration of Justice in Medieval India," highlights the evolution of a policing system of India that was subject to experimentation with various models during the process of conquest by foreign rulers. The Aryan system was supplanted by the Muslim legal system after the Muslim rulers embarked on a more permanent stay in India. The Muslim legal system could not be implemented in its original orthodox form. In order to be incorporated into the Indian setting, the Mughal emperors had to adapt the Muslim law to the Indian environment. The Panchayati system of India in combination with the Arab and Persian systems of the Delhi Sultanates and the Mughal Emperors respectively created a very versatile and unique administrative blend. Chapter 5, examines the system of policing and administration of justice during the Mughal period (1526–1707). It postulates that the Perso–Arab system that the Mughals inherited through the Delhi Sultanates was in turn transformed when this system came into contact with the multiracial and multireligious Indian environment. The new system went through a profound change when coming into contact with Indian society, institutions, and culture. The legal system and the policing system employed by the Mughals incorporated elements of Indian law and administration. The resulting system ended up as one that can be more accurately characterized as a blend of the Arab–Persian–Indian system of administration. The system was forced to adopt a very liberal and tolerant interpretation of the Muslim law. Mughal power began to wane when the policy changed to a more orthodox Sunni model under Aurangzeb.

Chapter 6, "Policing Muslim Community in India," highlights the problems Muslims, the largest minority of India, face as a consequence of discrimination and poor service from police in the country. The police tend to profile Muslim youth as terrorists in extremist-affected areas or involved in organized criminal activities in other regions. Examples of Muslims suffering from police action or worse, omission, are well documented. Muslims generally have low confidence in the Indian police and are unwilling to cooperate with them even when victimized. The chapter highlights the mutual suspicion that exists between the police and minority communities and points to its dangerous implications for internal security. However, the mistreatment of the Muslim community is also due to the internal problems of police administration. The chapter describes a variety of poor management practices debilitating the organization and prevailing indifference of the leadership towards performance appraisal. Even though it is well understood that the minorities are estranged, little systematic efforts are undertaken to address this problem. The alienation of Muslims can be addressed and minimized by not only encouraging greater recruitment of Muslims into the police services but also by addressing their specific problems. The police need to build greater trust among the community, which is linked to the provision of basic security to Muslims. Above all, the police need to become accountable to the people and involve them as coproducers of their own safety. A repressive ruler-oriented police, cannot serve the interests of minorities in a democratic society.

There are three main ways of overcoming the problems facing the Muslim community with respect to the police. First, open up the policing system to greater participation to Muslims. Special efforts should be made to employ young men and women from the Muslim community, so as to gradually reduce the predominance of anti-Muslim policy makers in this area.

Second, one should not tolerate incidents of blatant racism in police training, practices, or policy. Those who practice such racism should be ferreted out and removed from the force.

Finally, there must be recognition of the fact that as long as racism is present in the larger society, attempts to eradicate it from the criminal justice system will only have marginal success. So long as some religious groups are unfairly targeted and excluded from opportunities, there will be less likelihood of obeying the laws and the entire police apparatus would be looked upon as adversarial.

Chapter 7, "Policing Minorities in the Arab World," addresses the manner in which the police interact with their minorities which, essentially, depends on the nation's particular historical, legal, social, political, and religious characteristics. Research on the relationship between police and minorities in the Arab world merits scrupulous analysis, but has not received the required consideration. During the last two centuries, the Arab world remained the focus of European colonial powers and as such continued to be an area of deconstruction and experimentation in the criminal justice realm of the colonial administration. As a result, the current mixture of legal traditions in the Arab world emerges as an interesting area of study in examining the often-troubled relationship between police and minorities. With the exception of Lebanon, which has a sizeable non-Muslim population and an arrangement of power sharing among the different religious communities, all other Arab police forces comprise a vast majority of Muslims. This chapter attempts to explore some of the strategies various Arab governments are using in policing their minorities. Case studies of Egypt, Lebanon, and Saudi Arabia examine how distinct minorities are handled by the criminal justice system and police in these particular Muslim-dominated societies. These countries provide examples of policing by Muslim officers of their minorities.

Chapter 8, "Policing Muslims in a 'Combat/Peace' Environment: the Case of 'Policing by Religion' in Israel" highlights the dilemma of policing Muslim minorities by Muslim minorities and/or by police officers from a religiously mixed background operating out of a specialized, "Minority Unit" that experiences a number of mutations over more than four decades of "combat/peace" environments, where the Muslim population was and is frequently seen, informally, as the "enemy within" and the dilemma of equitable policing is shadowed by an inherent suspicion and the realities of possible collaboration with the "enemy." The desire to separate policing Muslim minorities as part of the Israeli society from the politically motivated terrorist activities which some of the community members have and might be involved in creates a tremendous challenge for the Israel National Police.

Chapter 9, "Pathways Towards an Equity and Parity in Policing," summarizes the attempts made by the authors to examine functional Muslim societies and the political apparatus employed to police Muslim communities and the cooperative arrangements that have yielded results when working partnerships have been established with Muslims elites who have been co-opted and have lent their support in the policing enterprise.

While examining the current paradigms and discourse of policing in Muslim societies and of Muslim communities the final chapter attempts to address the following future research questions.

• Which policies and practices have been effective in policing Muslim societies?
• What have been the merits/demerits of the different policing strategies and approaches?
• In which sociopolitical contexts have certain policing strategies proven to be effective?

- Do the training practices address and sensitize recruits on issues of human rights, community mobilization, and cultural and religious sensitivity?
- What are the models, if any, that need to be followed to address concerns of Muslim communities, especially with regard to terrorism related social anxieties?

The final paragraphs of the book are devoted to the "policing by religion" concept and its future applicability to effective law enforcement. History has shown that policing groups based on their religious affiliations is not the way to alleviate concerns of the given minority groups. Yet, removing politics from policing and police from politics, the way Sir Robert Peel, the founder of the Metropolitan Police Force, asserted his desire in 1829, remains a very distant and elusive goal of police profession reformers. Policing is a very politically infused profession (Haberfeld 2002). Religion and politics, no matter how much separated, if separated, remain as such only in a formal manner, as in the case of the Turkish police, that is addressed in the final chapter, yet on an individual and informal level this separation rarely produces the desired results. The future of policing Muslim communities is very deeply entrenched in history, politics and the current events and its progress is very much dependent upon more tolerance, more understanding, and more research regarding this deeply complex phenomenon. According to the most recent projection by the PEW Forum on Religion and Public Life, the Muslim population is forecast to grow at about twice the rate of the non-Muslim population over the next two decades, making up about 26.4% of the world's total projected population of 8.3 billion in 2030 (PEW Research Center 2012). One cannot afford to ignore the significance of these numbers and its impact on the way law enforcement is delivered to, by, and with the Muslim communities. This book is one of the first attempts to tackle a highly important and very sensitive topic that mandates much future scientific inquiry, that these authors hope to spark.

References

ACLU. (2012). Government Confirms That It Has Secret Interpretation of Patriot Act Spy Powers. http://www.aclu.org/blog/tag/patriot-act. Accessed April 11 2012.

Associated Press. (2011). *Highlights of AP's probe into NYPD intelligence operations.* http://ap.org/nypd/. Accessed 12 Feb 2011.

Cincotta, T. (2012). *Manufacturing the Muslim menace. Private firms, public servants, and the threat to rights and security.* Somerville: Political Research Associates.

Deepa, K. (2012). The NYPD: Islamophobia in blue. http://empirebytes.com/2012/02/06/the-nypd-islamophobia-in-blue/. Accessed 6 Feb 2012.

Haberfeld, M. R. (2002). *Critical issues in police training.* Upper Saddle River: Prentice Hall.

Patel, F., & E. Goitein (2012). It's time to police the NYPD. *New York Times.* Editorial dated 29 Jan 2012.

PEW Research Center. (2012). *The future of the global Muslim population.* http://pewforum.org/The-Future-of-the-Global-Muslim-Population.aspx. Accessed 5 Feb 2012.

Religious Profiling: Documents show NYPD recommended increased surveillance of Shiite Muslims. http://www.huffingtonpost.com/2012/02/03/religious-profiling-nypd_n_1252015.html. Accessed 5 Feb 2012.

Chapter 2
The Concept of Punishment Under Sharia

Islamic Law: Sharia is the code of conduct followed by Muslims and has its basis in two main sources: the Quran and the Sunnah of the Prophet. It seeks to foster success and welfare of humanity in both this life and in the afterlife. The Sharia prescribes a complete code of laws to guide mankind towards establishing good (Maruf) and removing evil (Munkar) from society. The Quran is the main source of the Sharia and lays out the main principles. The Sunnah provides guidance for the application of the principles that are laid down in the Quran. There are other sources of the Sharia-Ijma and Qiyas. Ijma (consensus) can be applied when there is no clear conclusion that can be derived from the Quran or the Sunnah. Qiyas (analogical reasoning) is arrived at through a process of deduction by comparing it with a similar situation in the past. Sharia is the outcome of a continuous process of development during the 14 centuries of the existence of Islam. According to classical theory, the Sharia consists of express injunctions of the Quran, the legislation introduced through the practice of the Prophet, and the opinions of jurists.

The Sharia is not a systematic code, but rather, a living and growing organism. There is a large degree of agreement among its different schools, inasmuch as the starting point and the basic principles are identical. The differences in approach have been occasioned due to economic, political, historical, and cultural factors. The Sharia is so intimately connected to religion that it cannot easily be severed from it (Gobind Dayal v. Inayatullah 1885:7 All. 775, 781). Sharia refers to the canon law of Islam, and comprises the totality of Allah's commandments. Each of these are referred to as hukm (pl. ahkam). This sacred law and its inner meaning is not easy to understand; it encompasses all human actions. As such, it is not law, in the modern sense, but rather, an infallible ethical guide. It consists of a fundamental doctrine of duties (Hurgronje 2010) and a code of obligations. Legal considerations and individual rights are secondary; instead it gives supreme importance to a religious evaluation of all the affairs of daily life.

F.B. Hakeem et al., *Policing Muslim Communities: Comparative International Context*, DOI 10.1007/978-1-4614-3552-5_2, © Springer Science+Business Media New York 2012

The Islamic conception of the law is an expression of the Divine will. Upon the death of the Prophet Muhammad, PBUH[1] the transmissions of the Divine will ceased, and as such the terms of the Divine revelation were considered to be fixed and immutable. After the process of interpretation and expansion, the source materials were held to be complete. The crystallization of the doctrine in the medieval legal manuals resulted in Sharia law becoming a rigid and static system. As opposed to secular legal systems, which grew out of society and changed with the changing circumstances of society, Sharia law was imposed upon society from above. Under Muslim law, it is not society that molds and fashions the law, but rather the law that precedes and controls society. Because the law is considered divine it is accepted as it is.

Schools of Islamic Law: Theories of Islamic law developed during the second century after the Hijra (i.e., around 800 CE). There were different schools of thought and each school was based on the writings of scholars dealing with different aspects of Islamic criminal law. These schools were based on the different interpretations of the Quran and Hadith, views of good and evil, and the varied socioeconomic and political circumstances.

The followers of Islam are divided into two main divisions: Sunni and Shia. Each of these is further subdivided into a number of schools, having their own authoritative texts. There are four schools of Sunnite law, which follow the four great jurists (Imam Abu Hanifa, Malik Ibn Anas, Ahmad Ibn Hanbal, and Muhammad Ibn Idris al-Shafeii). The followers of any of the Sunnite Schools may adopt any one of the four jurists as their guide. However, the teachings of the jurist must be followed consistently (Tyabji 1968). There are two authoritative texts of this school: these are the *Fatawa Alamgiri*, and the *Hedaya*. Both these texts were translated into English in the early nineteenth century.

As far as the Shia schools are concerned, these arose due to dynastic troubles and disputes regarding the person entitled to succeed as the rightful Imam. General Shia law had already been settled before these disputes and troubles. The main Shia School of jurisprudence is the Jafari School, which is named after the sixth Shia imam, Jafar al-Sadiq (699–765 CE). There are no differences in the basic beliefs of Islam, especially between Shias and Sunnis. Both believe in the five pillars of Islam. Over centuries a whole body of different rituals, and also forms of prayer have evolved. Much of this is only marginally different from the Sunni practice; one of the major differences is the Shia concept of Imamate versus the Sunni concept of Caliphate. The Shia tradition believes that the Imam must be a descendant of the Prophet. This concept of descent of the Prophet thus sets up a hereditary class hierarchy in the Imamate tradition of the Shias. As opposed to this tradition the Sunni tradition of Caliphate considers hereditary class succession alien to the spirit of Islam. For the Sunnis, matters and decisions among the Muslims should be governed by consensus. According to the Sunnis the Shia tradition of Imamate runs contrary to the principles of equality and consensus and thus has been rejected since the seventh century CE (Bassiouni 1982). However, with respect to the theory of punishment all schools agree with the main concepts. Differences stem from the interpretation and application of theory.

Category	Injunction	Actions
FARD	Strictly enjoined	Five daily prayers
MANDUB	Advisory (positive)	Performing additional prayers on Eid
JAIZ	Indifferent – Permitted	Travel by land, sea or air
MAKRUH	Advisory (negative)	Eating some kinds of fish
HARAM	Strictly prohibited	Alcohol consumption

Fig. 2.1 Religious injunctions

Islamic System of Criminal Law: Sharia means right path, or guide (Kamali 1999); it indicates the path to righteousness. Sharia is mostly contained in divine revelation such as the Quran and the Hadith. It comprises the totality of guidance that God revealed to the Prophet Muhammad regarding the dogma of Islam, its moral values, and its practical legal rules. The Sharia differs from Western systems of law on the basis of its scope and its conception of the law. According to Schacht (1964), the sacred law of Islam is an all-embracing body of religious duties, the totality of Allah's commands that regulate the life of every Muslim in all aspects. The scope of the Sharia is much wider, because it regulates an individual's relationship not only with one's neighbors and the state but also with God and one's conscience. Ritual practices such as *Salat* (prayer*), Zakat* (charity*), Saum (*fasting*), and Hajj* (pilgrimage*)* are an integral part of Sharia law. The Sharia deals with ethical standards as much as it does with legal rules, indicating not only what humans are entitled or bound to do in law, but also what they ought, in conscience, to do or refrain from doing. According to Sharia, actions are divided into five categories (see Fig. 2.1); these are referred to as al-akham al khamsa by Faruki (1966). *Fard* is a category that consists of acts that are strictly enjoined upon believers; these are compulsory duties and omission of these duties is liable to be punished. *Haram* consists of those activities that are strictly forbidden, and a violator is liable to be punished according to the law. Between these two extremes there are two middle categories. *Mandub* refers to actions that one is advised to do; these actions are rewarded but omission of these actions is not subject to punishment. *Makruh* refers to acts one is advised to refrain from doing; these actions are disliked or disapproved by the Sharia but not punished. The last category is *Jaiz*, which refers to actions about which religion is indifferent and thus permitted. Because the Sharia encompasses all human activity, it is necessary to understand this fivefold classification. This classification makes a distinction between acts that are morally enjoined and those that are legally enforceable. Because moral obligations differ from legal obligations, this distinction must be observed or else it could lead to error and confusion. This point was duly enunciated by Justice Mehmood in Gobind Dayal v. Inayatullah (1885) 7 All. 775, 805.

The Sharia is not merely a system of law, but also a comprehensive code of conduct that encompasses the public and private domains of an individual's activities. As opposed to the other systems of law the Sharia operates within the internal and external domains of an individual (inner conscience and external social relations). Through interplay of rituals, beliefs, actions, and community consciousness the individual is sought to be controlled.

Goals	Mechanisms	Techniques
Life	Islamic conscience; severe punishment	Qisas
Reputation	Islamic conscience; severe punishment	Hadd
Religion	Islamic conscience; severe punishment	Hajj; Tauhid; Saum; Salat, Zakat
Family	Islamic conscience; severe punishment	Hadd, Salat, Saum
Property	Islamic conscience; severe punishment; economic reform	Zakat

Fig. 2.2 Penal scheme of Sharia

The Islamic penal laws flow from the Quran and are supplemented by the Hadith. Although this law is based on divine sources, it is a living body of law that looks after the needs of Islamic society. Contrary to the common perception that is widely prevalent, Islamic laws are essentially preventive and are not based solely on harsh punishment as a first resort; rather the harsh punishments are implemented as a last resort. Because faithful Muslims internalize the values and mores of Islamic society, they are inclined to respect the rights of others and also perform their duties. As a consequence, the harsh punishments prescribed by the Sharia are rarely in need of being applied. The five famous goals of the Sharia are the protection of life, mind (reputation or feelings of the individual), religion, ownership, and family. Although it has not been mentioned thus in the Quran or the Hadith, Muslim jurists agree upon these goals. The agreement is derived through deduction from all the judgments of the relevant Islamic legal sources (Shatibi n.d.; Abuzahrah 1974; Al-Ghazzali 1894). The varied prohibitions and obligations in the Sharia were prescribed for attaining these ends. The ruler or other constituted authority of a state is required to act in the public interest to protect these five basic aspects of social life. The Sharia considers transgression against any one of these unlawful and therefore punishable. Figure 2.2 depicts the penal scheme employed by the Sharia. It delineates the goals, mechanisms, and techniques that are employed by the Sharia to safeguard society.

In order to achieve the above goals the Sharia adopts a policy that covers three different areas. According to Hathout (1997) the Sharia protects society from crime through three mechanisms: Islamic conscience, economic reform, and severe punishment.

(a) The establishment of the *Islamic Conscience* acts as a social force to reduce crime. It rests on the basis that Allah is omnipresent. The individual's family rearing, educational system, the media, and the general moral environment of the community influence this conscience. This mechanism helps to inculcate and internalize the values of Muslim society and acts as a built-in restraint on crime.

(b) Economic Reform: The Sharia seeks to address the material causes that lead to crime. It attempts comprehensive economic reform to address the needs of all members of society, so as to distribute wealth more equitably. This can be regarded as one of the ultimate responses to crime prevention. The institution of charity (*Zakat*) seeks to usher in economic reform.

(c) Severe Punishment. No punishment will deter others unless it is severe enough. Punishment serves the purposes of justice and assures the safety of the community. Society is assured that no one can commit a crime and get away with it.

An examination of the Islamic penal complex reveals that it has many highly interconnected institutions that need further analysis. Islam being a complete system for regulating all aspects of human life, the Sharia complements this system through maintenance of the essential institutions of *Hajj, Saum, Zakat, Tauhid,* and *Salat.* The rules, obligations, injunctions, and prohibitions stemming from the Quran and Hadith produce a complete picture of the ideal Muslim community (Ummah). According to some scholars of Islamic law (Souryal et al. 1994), Islamic justice is based on the philosophical principles that are regarded as alien, if not unconscionable, to the Western observer. The most prominent among these is the penalty of hand amputation for the offense of theft. In order to understand these practices, they should be examined within the socioreligious context of Islam and in the spirit of true theoretical inquiry. The imposition of this penalty in certain cases and under the stringent rules of evidence may be justifiable, and even necessary, within the Islamic context of sustaining a spiritual and peaceful society. Although this penalty is designed primarily as an instrument of social deterrence, its continuing and undisguised application acts as a potent reminder to the believers' spiritual obligation towards God and society. The use of this penalty does not seem to be inconsistent with the principles of natural law or the Judeo-Christian doctrine in their original versions. It has parallels to the other theological views of crime and punishment that were prevalent in the early Christian and Jewish traditions. According to the Old Testament, murder, willful assault on parents, or cursing parents, was punished with death by stoning. However, there were checks to the harsh provisions of the *lex talionis.* Believers were expected to exercise mercy on the errant members of their fold (Hoekema 1986). In this same vein the Sharia also has provisions for mercy, penance, and forgiveness.

According to some scholars (Garland 1991), the sociological approach to punishment offers a unique framework for the analysis of penal issues. Instead of treating punishment as a means to an end or a routine problem for moral philosophy, historians and sociologists regard punishment as a social institution. Through this perspective, punishment is regarded as a historical and cultural artifact that is not concerned merely with the control of crime but is also shaped by an array of social forces that have many further ramifications. This tradition examines the social bases of punishment. It delineates the social implications of specific penal modes, and seeks to uncover the structures of social action and the mesh of cultural meaning that gives modern punishment its distinctive forms, functions, and effects (Ignatieff 1978; Garland and Young 1983; Jacobs 1983; Cohen 1985; Hirst 1986). Here we examine penality under the Sharia from such a sociological perspective and focus on its many interconnected structures, processes, and distinctive functions. Through its interaction with sociocultural forces it has developed its own unique system of criminal justice.

Theory of Punishment Under Sharia: This theory of punishment derives from Divine law, which is contained in the Quran and the Hadith. It contains the basics of the rules and commands expressed generally. According to Muslims, the Quran is considered to be the word of God; it contains about 30 equal parts (*Paras*), divided into 114 chapters (*Suras*) and about 6,241 verses (*Aayats*). On the whole the Quran has very little legislative material, with only about 10% of its verses containing rules. About 200 verses of the Quran deal with legal issues.[2] According to Pearl (1987), the Sharia consists of Quranic legislation that was later interpreted by subsequent generations and incorporated much of the customary law of the Arabs. Strictly speaking the Quran provides the laws that were given by the divine authority: Allah. Islamic law is a divinely ordained system of commands. Denying these laws would amount to a renunciation of the Muslim religion (Lippman et al. 1988). In order to settle issues Muslims have developed a detailed legal system whereby complex issues can be examined, compared with known Islamic teachings, and then evaluated. This is referred to as the science of Fiqh (understanding the legal positions). Thus Sharia is the path of living Islam and Fiqh is the process employed to apply it. Because all Muslims do not agree on everything, there are different traditions of Fiqh, each with its own methods of research and interpretation.

Classification of Crimes: Under the Sharia, punishment can be classified under three main categories: *Al-Hudud* (fixed punishments), *Al-Qisas* (restitutory), and *Al-Taazir* (discretionary). Islamic law has many similar defenses to crime as in the common law nations, including the use of puberty as the age of accountability. The penal philosophies under the Islamic system are similar to the Western views in theory, but they are applied in very different ways. Many punishments under the Sharia are public and are carried out as a deterrent to others. Sharia judges have much more freedom in sentencing options than Western judges. They have mandatory sentences for only a few of the most serious *Hadd* crimes. Some critics in the popular media point to the harshness of Islamic law and conclude that it must be wrong. However, scholars aver that Islamic law is not wrong but merely different (Wiechman et al. 1995). Figure 2.3 details the forms and purpose of the Sharia. It deals with the goals of the Sharia and delineates the forms and purpose for each kind of punishment and the sentencing options available to the judge.

Forms	Purpose	Options
Hadd	Deterrence; retribution; expiation	None; mandatory
Qisas	Restitution	Some; limited
Taazir	Reform; deterrence	Full discretion of judge/authority

Fig. 2.3 Goals of punishment under Sharia

Al-Hudud (Fixed Punishments)

The word *Hadd* (pl. *Hudud*) implies punishment that has been prescribed by God in the Quran or the Hadith. Crimes for which the Quran names certain fixed punishments are called *Hudud*. These are few, and like the rituals, are constant and unchanging. The application of this punishment is the right of God (*Haqq Allah*). Religious obligations such as prayer, fasting, and hajj are classified as *Haqq Allah*, the pure right of God, and are normally not justiciable. *Haqq adami* or the right of human beings such as debt repayment and spousal support are rights that can be made the subject of a judicial order. Under Islamic law duties and obligations may be categorized as the right of humans (*Haqq adami*) and the right of God (*Haqq Allah*). *Haqq Allah* is the punishment prescribed by God and revealed in the Quran/Hadith and its application is the right of God (*Haqq Allah*).

Hadd punishments have three main purposes: retribution against the wrongdoer for contravening the laws of society, expiation for the culprit after the punishment has been inflicted, and as a general and specific deterrent. According to Mawardi (1380 A.H.) deterrence is recognized as the main justification for *Hadd* punishments. Mawardi defined *Hudud* as being deterrent punishments that were established by God in order to prevent human beings from committing what He forbade and from neglecting what He commanded.

The main features of this type of punishment are that:

1. This punishment is prescribed in the public interest.
2. The punishment cannot be adjusted in any manner, that is, either lightened or made heavier.
3. After being reported to the judge (Qazi) it cannot be pardoned by anyone: judge, victim, or political authority.

This conceptualization of punishment is somewhat similar to the conscience collective mentioned by Durkheim (1947). After the law has been broken, punishment should be meted out without fear or favor or it would lead to a crumbling of the social fabric. The permanence of Hadd punishments is mirrored in the following verse of the Quran: *II: 229, Sura Al-Baqarah:*

These are the limits imposed by Allah. Transgress them not. For whoso transgresseth Allah's limits: such are wrongdoers (Pickthall 1992; Khan 1979; Ali 1983).

Under Islamic criminal law six major offenses are recognized as *Hudud*. Penalties for each of these offenses have been prescribed in the Quran (and the Hadith).

Classification: *Hadd* offenses may be classified into six categories: (a) *Al-Sariqa* (theft), (b) *Al-Hiraba* (armed robbery), (c) *Al-Zina* (illicit sexual relations), (d) *Al-Qadhf* (slanderous accusation of unchastity), (e) *Shurb al-Khamr* (drinking alcohol), and (f) *Al-Ridda* (apostasy). For an offense to be categorized as *Hadd*, it should be established that the punishment for it is determined in fixed terms in the Quran and the Hadith. According to El-Awa (1984) only four of the six offenses may be classified as offenses of *Hudud*. The other two (alcohol drinking and apostasy), cannot be so categorized because neither of these calls for punishment that is strictly defined by the Quran and the Hadith. However, according to Doi (1997), a seventh category also needs to be added, *Al-Firar Min Al-Zahf* (running away from the battlefield during Jihad) and is also liable to *Hadd* punishment. Many other scholars disagree with this categorization.

AL-QISAS

The punishment prescribed under Islamic law for murder and personal injury is known as *Qisas* or *Qawad* (retaliation). This means the infliction of injury on a culprit that is exactly equal to the injury that was inflicted on the victim. Islamic law gives preference to the wronged individual's wishes when administering *Qisas*. This feature distinguishes it from the procedure adopted for homicide under modern legal systems. Though homicide appears to be a tort (Anderson 1951) under Islamic law, this is not an accurate categorization. According to some scholars (Shaltut 1964; El-Awa 1984) the punishment for homicide under the Sharia has a dual nature. It is regarded as a crime for which punishment is imposed and as a tort, which compels the perpetrator to pay compensation, so that the victim may benefit. The ancient Arabs considered the concept of punishment inflicted by the state for homicide as an innovation of Islam. However, Islam did not completely abolish the pre-Islamic conception of punishment.

The law of *Qisas* can be understood after looking at the ancient customs of the Arabs prior to the advent of Islam. Hostility was a characteristic feature of the tribesmen of pre-Islamic Arabia. Friendly co-operation was a way of life only among the members of the same tribe. The main feature for this state of hostility was personal revenge for homicide. One of the most compelling reasons for the motive of revenge among Arab tribesmen was their belief that after the death of a murdered person a night-bird known as *Ham*, would stand on the grave and cry, "I am thirsty, give me a drink." This implied that revenge should be taken in order to quench its thirst. As a consequence, revenge was taken not only against the culprit, but also against the culprit's tribesmen. On many occasions tribal pride called for several victims as an equivalent for a fellow tribesman; this was the same with respect to the infliction of injury. *Diya* (blood money) was considered as a peaceful alternative to revenge. However, the amount of *Diya* varied according to the status of the murderer and his or her tribe. After Islam prevailed in Arabia the law of *Qisas* was introduced. As a consequence, just retaliation allowed only one life, that of the perpetrator of the crime only, to be taken for the life of the victim, or a fixed sum of money was determined as blood money. This was not to vary from tribe to tribe or due to the status of the victim. At this stage the Quranic law radically changed the legal incidents of homicide (Coulson 1964). There was a transition from the pre-Islamic custom of *Thar* (revenge) to the Islamic law of *Qisas*.

The punishment for homicide and bodily injury in Islamic law can be either *Qisas* (retaliation) or *Diya* (blood money). *Qisas* can be divided into two categories: *Qisas* for homicide and *Qawad* for wounds or injuries. *Diya* signifies the blood money owed for killing and the term *Arash* is used for the blood money owed for injuries. *Diya* and *Kaffara* (penance) are the remedies for accidental homicide. The punishment prescribed in the Quran for deliberate homicide is the killing of the culprit or the payment of *Diya*. With respect to accidental homicide the jurists have determined that no *Qisas* is owed but the perpetrator is responsible for *Diya* and *Kaffara* (penance). Unlike retaliation for homicide the law regarding retaliation for injuries was not clearly prescribed in the Quran or the Hadith. Even the verses of the Quran on which the jurists based the law of retaliation for injuries are subject to interpretation. With regard to the Hadith, there is only one report where the Prophet ordered retaliation for injuries; Imam Bukhari and Muslim transmitted this through their compilations of the traditions.

The law of *Qisas* for injuries is not set out by the Quran and the Hadith but is based on *Ijma* (consensus). Jurists since the time of the Prophet are in agreement concerning this.

The following conditions have to exist before the law of Qisas for injuries applies: The injury must be deliberate (*Amd*) and not accidental (*Khata*), the part of the body where *Qisas* can be applied must be the same as the part injured by the culprit, and it must be practicable for the authority to inflict *Qisas*.

According to the Maliki and Shafeii jurists, if all these conditions exist then *Qisas* must be inflicted. However the jurists from the Hanafi school are of the view that *Qisas* for injuries can only be administered in two cases: when the injury reaches the skull bone (*al-muwaddaha*) and for an articular injury (*al-jinaya ala-mifsal*).

Diya is the only punishment for quasi-deliberate homicide. In cases of deliberate homicide it is due only when the nearest relatives of the victim do not insist on *Qisas* against the culprit.

Sharia scholars classify homicide into various categories and these differ from one school to another and also between jurists belonging to the same school. The Hanafi School gives five types of classifications: *Amd* (deliberate), *Shabah al-Amd* (quasi-deliberate), *Khata* (accidental), *Jari majra al-Khata* (equivalent to acciden-tal), and *Bisabab* (indirect). Only the first category calls for the infliction of Qisas, whereas the remedy for all the others is Diya. These classifications came into vogue for the Hanafi School after al-Jassas (1928), the famous Hanafi jurist. The Shafeii, Hanbali, and Zaydi Schools have only three categories: deliberate, quasi-deliberate, and accidental. The Maliki and Zahiri schools have two categories: deliberate and accidental.

The law of *Diya* for injuries is very complex. According to the Sharia nearly every part of the body has been considered with respect to the amount of *Diya* or

Arash, which is due upon injury. If there is no fixed amount that has been determined then the victim is entitled to compensation known as *hukumat adl*, which is an amount of money determined by the judge and paid to the victim. Most of the jurists are in agreement that blood money (*Diya* or *Arash*) can replace retaliation when it is not possible to inflict or when the matter has been amicably settled. The victim has the choice to pick from a variety of options. The Sharia is victim-centered because the victim has three options: pardon the offender, ask the offender for Diya, or ask the State to enforce the death sentence against the culprit.

Taazir

This form of punishment seeks to prevent crime, encourage respect for society, and reform the offender. In Islamic legal writings the word *Taazir* signifies a punishment that seeks to prevent the criminal from further committing crimes and secondly at reforming the criminal. It therefore has a dual purpose, to deter and to reform. Ibn Farhun (1301 A.H.) in his famous book *Tabsirat al-Hukkam* delineates the aims of *Taazir* to be a sort of disciplinary, reformative, and deterrent type of punishment.

Taazir was defined as a form of discretionary punishment that was to be delivered for transgression against God, or against an individual for which neither fixed punishment nor penance was prescribed (Sarakhsi 1342 A.H.). This definition therefore excludes all crime for which Qisas is prescribed, because in all cases where *Hadd, Kaffara*, or *Qisas* are applied, *Taazir* cannot be applied to replace them.

The word *Taazir* was not used in the Quran or the Hadith in the sense that the Muslim jurists use it. However, the Quran and the Hadith referred to some categories of crimes for which no fixed punishments were prescribed. It was left to the judge or the ruler to decide what type or manner of punishment should be imposed. There are three instances where the Quran mentions this type of punishment: An-Nisa (women) verses 16, 34 and Al-Shura (consultation) verse 40. One of the relevant verses of the Quran refers to the punishment for homosexuality. It orders the authority "to punish them both," but the type of punishment is not given and it is left entirely up to the judge. Rulers and judges are facilitated in safeguarding the interests of society when these are threatened by actions or omissions that fall beyond the purview of *Hadd* and *Qisas*.

Though it was not used in the Quran or the Hadith, it is not correct to say that the Quran does not know about this kind of punishment. In fact the Quran lays down the general principles from which *Taazir* was deduced and further mentions some of its applications. The legal principles of Taazir are implied in the Quran. Examples and cases of *Taazir* are also found in the Hadith. These cases were used later in a manner to construct the juristic formulation of *Taazir* as part of the Sharia. The jurists owe their knowledge of *Taazir* to the Hadith of the Prophet. The decisions of the companions regarding *Taazir* are more clearly enunciated in the manuals of Islamic law; however, they were still based on the Hadith of the Prophet.

The punishments for *Taazir* are not determinate. The judge has wide discretion in such cases. The judge can choose the punishment that is most suitable to a particular crime, or the circumstances of the criminal, her prior conduct, and his psychological condition. However, the judge does not have unfettered or unbridled authority and is obliged not to order a punishment that is not permitted under the Sharia. For example, he cannot order that the offender be whipped naked.

These punishments are not the only ones that can be prescribed in cases of *Taazir*. Any punishment that serves the purpose of *Taazir*, that is, to prevent any further crime and reform the offender, can be used so long as it does not contradict the general principles of Islamic law. The punishments meted out under *Taazir* represent what was known and actually used in Islamic legal texts and practice; however, any other type of useful punishment may also be legally employed. Besides determining the punishment, the ruler or Qazi (judge) is also traditionally given the task of determining whether an act is criminal. This is the essence of *Taazir*, which has been defined as a punishment for any transgression. Because transgressions cannot be foreseen, this right has been granted to the ruler or Qazi to meet the needs of society and protect it against all kinds of transgressions.

Kinds of Taazir: There are ten different kinds of *Taazir* according to the Sharia and these vary in level of severity. They range from a mere admonition right up to the death penalty.

1. Admonition (*Al Waz*). Under this category the person committing the transgression is reminded that he or she has done an unlawful thing. According to the Quran (IV:34 An-Nisa) it was provided as the first stage in dealing with disobedient wives. It is sought to be an admonition to remind the offender, that he or she has forgotten or is unaware of the fact that something wrong has been committed. This treatment is meant to be reserved for those who commit minor offenses for the first time, so long as the judge considers it sufficient to reform and restrain the culprit from any further transgression.
2. Reprimand (*Al-Tawbikh*): This kind of reprimand could be through any word or act which the judge feels is sufficient to serve the purpose of *Taazir*. The jurists refer to some specific words and acts as a means of reprimand. However, it is not necessary to dwell on these means because they vary according to the offense and the offender.
3. Threat (*Al-Tahdid*): This is a method through which the offender can be induced to improve her or his behavior out of fear of punishment. It may also comprise credible threats of punishment if the offense is repeated or by pronouncing a sentence against the culprit, the execution of this sentence is delayed until another offense has been committed within a stipulated time period. This method of dealing with offenders is comparable to the modern penal concept of suspended sentences, which exists under most modern penal systems. The period during which the sentence may be suspended is referred to as the *operational period* under the English Criminal Justice Act of 1967. This operational period cannot be less than 1 year or more than 3 years. Under the Islamic penal system this operational

period is left entirely up to the discretion of the judge. The second difference between the Islamic and the English system is that under English law the court has no power to suspend a sentence other than imprisonment. However, under Islamic law the judge has complete authority to suspend any kind of sentence.

4. Boycott (*Al-Hajr*): This form of *Taazir* punishment is prescribed in the Quran (IV: 34 An-Nisa). Besides being practiced by the Prophet it was imposed by Omar bin Khattab against a man who used to ask about and discuss difficult words in the Quran merely to confuse people and create mischief. Some scholars believe that this form of punishment is not practical in modern times.

5. Public Disclosure (*Al-Tashhir*): This type of punishment has been used since early Islamic times. Shurahyh, a famous judge who served under the Caliphs Omar and Ali, believed that the person giving false witness must be publicly identified so as to warn people not to trust him. All four Islamic schools are in agreement on this point. The method of public disclosure usually comprised taking the offender by the judge's representatives to every part of the city and announcing that he had committed an offense for which he had received a Taazir punishment. The purpose of this punishment was to inform the public that the offender was not to be trusted. In the present times the mode of public disclosure differs. Due to the advances in media for the dissemination of information, this can now be done by publishing the court judgment in the newspapers, or by broadcasting it on radio and television, or by any other method that informs the public regarding the offense (Ibn Farhun).

6. Fines and seizure (*Al-Gharamah wal-Musadarah*): Though the Prophet imposed financial penalties as *Taazir* punishments, the jurists are split into three groups regarding its legality. One group believes that it is illegal to punish by fine or by seizure of property; a second group considers it to be legal; a third group regards it as legal only if the offender does not repent. According to Imam Malik, Ahmad bin Hanbal, and Abu Yusuf and some of the Shafeii jurists, financial punishments are allowed as a *Taazir*. The judge or ruler should not take the offender's money or property for the public treasury but should merely keep it away from her until the culprit has shown repentance. No one is allowed to take another's money without legal reason (*Bisabab Shari*). Later on if it appears that the offender will not repent, the ruler is entitled to order that the money be spent for public purposes. The reason advanced for this explanation is that allowing a judge or ruler to take the offender's money for the public treasury could subject this practice to abuse by unjust judges or rulers. Those who deny the legality of Taazir punishment aver that it was legalized in the beginning of Islam but was abrogated later. The Hanafi jurist Tahawi was the first to advance this view in his famous book, *Sharh Ma'ani al-Athar*. Ibn Taymiyya, and his student, Ibn al-Qayyim, strongly reject this claim of abrogation. The other Hanbali, Hanafi, and Maliki commentators also hold this view and defend it. As per Ibn al-Qayyim's evidence, both elements of financial punishment are permitted in Islamic law. The statement made by the famous Orientalist, Schacht (1964) that there are no fines in Islamic law is therefore patently incorrect.

7. Imprisonment (*Al-Habs*): Under Islamic law there are two types of punishment; either for a definite term or for an indefinite term. Imprisonment for a definite term is imposed for minor offenses. The minimum duration of imprisonment is 1 day but the schools adopt different views regarding the maximum period of *Taazir* imprisonment. According to one group of schools (Hanafi, Maliki, and Hanbali), there is no maximum period specified for *Taazir* imprisonment. The period is indeterminate and varies by the offense and individual offender. As opposed to this view the Shafeii School sets a determinate period. The maximum period of imprisonment can be a month for investigation and 6 months as punishment. However, the total period of imprisonment cannot exceed 1 year. The majority view seems to favor an indeterminate period of imprisonment as punishment. This punishment can last until the criminal repents, or until his death if the person is a dangerous criminal (Ibn Farhun 1301 A.H.).

8. Banishment (*Al-Nafy*) is also a variant of this form of Taazir punishment. The Hanafi School applies this as an additional Taazir punishment for fornication. Along with the crime of fornication, banishment is regarded as a Taazir punishment and is administered to offenders who could encourage others to copy their deviant activities (Ibn Farhun 1301).

9. Flogging (*Al-Jald*): Flogging is a common form of punishment under the Sharia. It is referred to as the form of punishment for the crime of Qadhf (80 lashes) and for Zina committed by an unmarried person. The most liberal stance in this context is the one taken by the Maliki School, which avers that the Taazir punishment can exceed the Hadd punishment only as long as the judge or the ruler considers it necessary. The Zahiri and Zaydi Schools along with a section of the Hanbali School hold a contrary view that flogging, as a form of Taazir punishment cannot exceed 10 lashes. Another intermediate view is held by the Hanafi and Shafeii schools and by some Hanafi scholars. There is no unanimity about the maximum number of lashes. Furthermore, there is no consensus regarding the minimum number of lashes allowed as Taazir. Some jurists fix the minimum at three, but a majority does not agree with this view because it is at odds with the main feature of Taazir, which is its variation from one crime to another, according to the offender's character and other circumstances.

10. Death Penalty (*Al-Taazier bil Qatl*): Taazir punishments are meant to deal with the less serious offenses. The death penalty is normally imposed for the most serious crimes. According to the Sharia, it is the punishment stipulated for two *Hadd* offenses and as *Qisas*, for the crime of homicide. Normally, the jurists are against it being used as a *Taazir* punishment. However, in exceptional cases almost every school permits *Taazir* by death penalty. Examples of those who can be given the death penalty are mentioned in the Hanafi texts. The habitual homosexual, the murderer on whom *Qisas* cannot be imposed due to the means used in the crime, or the habitual thief who attacks a man's house and cannot be prevented from doing so by other punishments. With respect to the Maliki School, *Taazir* punishment is meant to fit the crime, the criminal and the victim and it is absolute in its application. The death penalty is permissible in certain cases where either the offense itself is very serious, such as spying for the

enemy, or propagating heretical doctrines, or practices which split the community, or if the criminal is an habitual offender whose wickedness can only be stopped by the death penalty. The Shafeii and the Hanbali Schools permit the death penalty to be imposed in the same cases for which it is permitted by the Malikis (Ibn-al Qayyim, in *Al-Turuq al-Hukmiyya*).

Notes

1. PBUH: all references to the Prophet Mohammed are followed by the words (pbuh) which means peace be upon him. When mentioning the name of the Prophet Muhammad, it is recommended that Muslims offer a prayer for him. The recitation – *salla Allahu alay hi wa sallam* (may God's peace and blessings be upon him) usually follows the Prophet's name when it appears in classical biographies. Since this book is intended for a much wider audience, which may include Muslims as well as non-Muslims, I shall omit mentioning it in the text, however, the devout Muslim reader can personally and inwardly recite this prayer when coming across the name of the Prophet.
2. The Quran makes references to legal matters in some verses. There are 114 chapters (Surahs) in the Quran. Each of the chapters is of variable length. In order to reference the relevant parts we will use the chapter and verse numbers within that chapter. For example, II: 286 will refer to verse 286 in the second chapter of the Quran, which is Al Baqarah (the cow). Some of the relevant verses of the Quran dealing with crime are as follows:
   Al-Sariqa (theft) II: 286; V: 38,39;
   Zina (fornication) XVII: 32; XXIV: 2–9;
   Shurb al-Khamr (intoxication) II: 219; V: 93;
   Al-Hiraba (highway robbery) V: 33,34; Killing (oath) II: 178,179; V: 33;
   Al-Qadhf (defamation) XXIV: 4,5,11,19,23,24;
   Witnesses II: 140,282,283; IV: 15,135; V: 8,108,111; XXIV: 13;
   Punishments II: 178,179; IV: 15,16,92,93; V: 36,37,41,42; XXIV:2–5;
   Taubah (repentance) IX: all verses particularly verse 29;
   Qisas (lawful retaliation) II: 178; V: 33–35,45; XLII: 39,40;
   War and peace II: 217; IV: 71,100; VIII: 41,61.
   Jihad VIII: 15–16

References

Ali, Y. A. (1983). *The holy Quran*. Brentwood: Amana Corp.
Anderson, J. N. (1951). Homicide in Islamic law. *Bulletin of the School of Oriental and African Studies, 13*, 811.
Bassiouni, M. C. (1982). *The Islamic criminal justice system*. New York: Oceana Publications.
Cohen, S. (1985). *Visions of social control: Crime, punishment and classification*. New York: Polity Press.

Coulson, N. J. (1964). *A history of Islamic law*. Edinburgh: Edinburgh University Press.
Doi, A. R. (1997). *Sharia: The Islamic law*. London: Taha Publishers.
Durkheim, E. (1947). *The division of labor in society*. Glencoe: Free Press.
El-Awa, M. S. (1984). *Punishment in Islamic law: A comparative study*. Indianapolis: American Trust Publications.
Faruki, K. (1966). *Al Ahkam al Khamisa. The five values*. Pakistan: JI Islamic Research Institute.
Garland, D. (1991). *Punishment and modern society*. Chicago: University of Chicago Press.
Garland, D., & Young, P. (1983). *The power to punish: Contemporary penality and social analysis*. Atlantic Highlands: Humanities Press.
Gobind Dayal v. Inayatullah, 1885: 7 All. 775, 781.
Hathout, M. (1997). Crime and punishment: an Islamic perspective. *Minaret, 19*: 9–11.
Hirst, P. Q. (1986). *Law, socialism and democracy*. London: Allen and Unwin.
Hoekema, D. (1986). Punishment and Christian social ethics. *Criminal Justice Ethics, 5*(2), 31–35.
Hurgronje, C. S. (2010). *Mohammedanism*. New York: General Books, LLC.
Ignatieff, M. (1978). *A just measure of pain. The penitentiary in the industrial revolution*. New York: Pantheon Books.
Jacobs, J. B. (1983). *New perspectives on prisons and imprisonment*. Ithaca: Cornell University Press.
Kamali, M. H. (1999). Law and society. The interplay of revelation and reason in the Sharia. In J. Esposito (Ed.), *The Oxford history of Islam*. New York: Oxford University Press.
Khan, M. M. (1979). *The translation of the meanings of Sahih al-Bukhari*. Chicago: Kazi.
Lippman, M. R., McConville, S., & Yerushalmi, M. (1988). *Islamic criminal law and procedure: An introduction*. New York: Praeger.
Pearl, D. (1987). *A textbook on Muslim personal law*. London: Croom Helm.
Pickthall, M. M. (1992). *The glorious Quran*. New York: Tahrike Tarsile Quran.
Schacht, J. (1964). *An introduction to Islamic law*. Oxford: The Clarendon Press.
Souryal, S. S., Potts, D. W., & Abobied, A. I. (1994). The penalty of hand amputation for theft in Islamic justice. *Journal of Criminal Justice, 22*(3), 249–265.
Tyabji, F. B. (1968). *Muslim law*. Bombay: N.M. Tripathi.
Wiechman, D. J., Azarian, M. K., & Kendall, J. D. (1995). Islamic courts and corrections. *International Journal of Comparative and Applied Criminal Justice, 19*(1), 33–46.

Arabic Sources

Abuzahrah, Muhammad (1974) Al-Jarimah wa Al-Uqubah Fi Al-Fiqh al-Islami (crime and punishment in Islamic Jurisprudence). Cairo: Dar al-Fikr al-Arabi.
Al-Ghazzali, Al-Mustafa (1894) Min Ilm Al usul. Cairo: al-Matbaah al-Amirugah.
Al-Jassas, Ahmad Ibn Ali (1928) Ahkam al-Quran (Quranic rules). Egypt: Al-Matbaah al-Bahiyah al Misriyah.
Ibn al-Qayyim al-Jawziyya (1961) Al Turuq al-Hukmiyya Fil-Siyasat al-Shariiya (Methods of judgment in a Sharia-oriented Policy). Cairo: al-Muassasa al-Arabiyya lil-Tabaa.
Ibn Farhun, Ibrahim Shams al-din Muhammad. (1301 A.H.) *Tabsirat al-Hukkam*. Cairo: al-Matbaah al-Bahiyah.
Mawardi, Ali bin Muhammad bin Habib (1380 A.H.) *Al Ahkam al-Sultaniya*. Cairo.
Shaltut, Shaikh Mahmud (1964) *Al-Islam, Aquida wa Sharia*. Cairo.
Sarakhsi, Muhammad bin Sahl (Abu Bakr) (1342 A.H.) *Kitab al-Mabsut*. Cairo: Matbaat al Saadah.
Abu Ishaq Ibrahim al-Shatibi, (n.d) al-Muwafaqat fi usul al-Ahkam (Concordances in the Essentials of Sharia Rulings), ed. Shaykh Abd Allah Diraz . Cairo: al Maktaba al-Tijariyya al kubra.
Tahawi, Ahmad bin Muhammad bin Salamah (1929) *Sharh Ma'ani al-Athar*. India.

Chapter 3
Policing Muslims in Western Democracies

Introduction

It is debatable if the world changed on September 11, 2001. What is true is that it changed perceptions about Muslims and has seriously affected the community in every democratic society. Although Muslims are present in every society in significant numbers, the scarf on the head, beard on the chin, and going to mosque, all are viewed with suspicion and alarm today. The ongoing conflicts in many regions where Muslims constitute a majority and continuing threats from terrorist groups proclaiming Islamic ideology add to these perceptions. The attacks on Muslim citizens in almost every democracy and hostility to their religious and cultural practices are becoming common too. Muslims feel harassment from security agencies and apprehend profiling from many other institutional actors. As a minority, Muslims perceive discrimination and lack of participation in the democratic polity like all other minorities. But after 911, Muslims have become the most visible minority and at the receiving end of disturbing discrimination in developed nations. Unfortunately, this holds true in all the western democracies where rule of law, protection of rights, and equality are prized and proclaimed ideals.

Although prejudices against minorities have existed for a long time a new form emerged after 911 attacks. This "Islamophobia" (Cainkar 2002; Spalek et al. 2008) has been seen in the growing victimization and attacks on Muslim people. A Pew survey (2007) reports that Muslims perceive that governments, both in the United Kingdom and the United States, have singled them out for government surveillance or law enforcement actions.

Even more specifically, a poll published in 2007 reflected that 53% of American Muslims feel it has been harder to be a Muslim in the USA since 9/11; 54% believe Muslims are singled out in government anti-terrorism efforts; 9% report being singled out by police; and 30% of those who have flown report being singled out by security personnel in airports (Silk 2010: 24).

Muslims in the United Kingdom since the terrorist attacks in London in 2005 (Abbas 2007; Khan 2009) and in European nations such as The Netherlands, after Theo van Gogh's murder in 2004 have felt severe antagonism from the majority community.

F.B. Hakeem et al., *Policing Muslim Communities: Comparative International Context,*   23
DOI 10.1007/978-1-4614-3552-5_3, © Springer Science+Business Media New York 2012

Background

Any discussion of Muslims in western systems must begin with a general survey about their proportionate numbers. According to a Pew Survey (2009) there are almost 35 million Muslims in Europe (including Russia). Of the approximately 4.6 million Muslims in the Americas, more than half, or about 2.5 million, live in the United States. But Canada has more than double the percentage of Muslims in the United States. Two percent of Canadians, about 700,000 people, are Muslim; in contrast, 0.8% of the U.S. population is Muslim. There are approximately 365,000 Muslims living in Australia forming 1.7% of the population of the country. Muslims number around 35,000 living in New Zealand forming 0.9% of the population. While the proportion of Muslims living in western style democracies is small the numbers, particularly those who are educated and enjoy economic prosperity are large. As such, Muslims do figure in public discussions and issues disproportionately to their percentage.

The "Problem" of Muslim Minorities

Ahmed (1993) says it is not difficult to see why Muslims who live as a minority in non-Muslim countries are seen by them as a problem. The reasons are partly due to historical and political factors, although the media have increasingly been playing an active role in displaying the Muslims as "others." An image is created that the Muslims are violent, unreliable, and prone to anarchy. Ahmed (1993) further argues that most non-Muslim countries in which Muslims are a small minority have an image of themselves as plural, tolerant, secular, and modern societies, but somehow the Muslims challenge this image. This stems largely from some issues about which Muslims are most sensitive. The most important is religion. Muslims like to visit their mosques and say their prayers without being questioned about these practices that are fundamental to their faith. They also like privacy in their homes (like any-one else) where they can lead their lives as Muslims. This implies they would like some control over their lives, some perpetuation of their own customs and values, the construction and maintenance of mosques which are the focus of social and cultural life, the capacity to read the Qur'an and the chance to live as Muslims and by Muslim traditions. These include family laws, inheritance, religious holidays, and religious festivals. When these are questioned and sometimes even threatened, Muslims are threatened; confusion and anger ensue (Ahmed 1993).

Whatever be the reasons, there is little doubt that "in the field of police-minority relations in deeply divided societies reveals that tense relations between the minority and the police are a frequent phenomenon" (Hasisi 2008: 1120). While political and social marginalization is an important factor the perceived discrimination towards their cultural practices and denial of equal opportunities form equally significant factors. These in turn raise questions about the legitimacy of the political order in the eyes of the minority that further aggravates the situation. This further leads to tense relations that often exist between police and minorities in various societies. There is evidence of high rates of minority arrest and incarceration, high rates of police violence towards minorities, and negative attitudes among minorities towards the police (Tyler 2005; Hasisi 2008). Furthermore, stereotypical images of minorities are prevalent among police officers. Most commonly, police view minority members as a potential criminal threat. On the other hand, a recurring complaint by the Muslim groups is that they are simultaneously over-policed as suspects and under-policed as victims, which has reduced their confidence in and willingness to collaborate with the police.

A peculiar dimension about policing of Muslims as minorities in western nations is the persisting notion of identity. "For many, including members of believer communities, being Western and being Muslim are two separate identities that cannot be habitually reconciled" (Canefe 2008: 391). Earlier, these societies could assimilate different identities that were ethnically and culturally dissimilar but nevertheless had two important factors in common: race and Christian faith, though defined and practiced with variation. In these societies differences were integrated or translated into functioning multicultural societies. The decision makers could revel in their senses and sensibilities of how variant their constitutive elements are from each other even though in comparison these were minor to the present-day societies. The post-Diaspora vision asserts that here and now things can and will change based on the new demands made by new generations of claims makers. In Canada, for example, it is no longer possible and reasonable to entertain that the French and the English people alone can claim what defines Canadianness and core Canadian values. The same holds true for the French, the Americans, the British, and even the Germans in the Western context, and numerous other societies in post-colonial and post-imperial circumstances. Despite such clear principles developing in western democracies the fact remains that Muslims in particular are at the receiving end of the law enforcement agencies.

Muslims in the United States

Haddad and Lummis (1987) divide the history of Muslims in the United States into two broad demographic categories: the immigrant and the indigenous. Immigrant Muslims consist of those whose parents, grandparents, or relatives originate from more than 80 countries around the world. Indigenous Muslims consist primarily of African Americans and now also include a growing number of Hispanics and Anglo converts to Islam. According to Leonard (2002) the indigenous population makes up the largest group of Muslims living in the United States consisting of more than 2.5 million people. They constitute roughly 30–42% of the estimated seven million Muslims residing in the United States (CAIR 2005 cited in Gaskew 2008: 43). South Asian and Arab nations provide the second and the third largest groups. Sub-Saharan Africans and Iranians make up 10%, the Turks 6% and other Asians around 5% (Nimer 2002).

Muslim migration to the United States occurred in several waves beginning in 1876 when several hundred Muslims from the Syrian region of the Ottoman Empire attended the Philadelphia International Exposition and settled down for financial reasons. The fall of the Ottoman Empire also encouraged a large number of Muslims to seek the refuge and opportunities of the United States, and Arab Muslims also migrated in large numbers after WWII when the oil industry built associations between the U.S. and Arab regions. Once President Johnson revoked the exclusion of Asian immigrants in 1965, Muslims from South Asia in particular added to the Muslim diaspora. Today, Muslim immigrants represent a mosaic of ethnic, national, religious, and ideological backgrounds (Haddad 2004).

Situation of Muslims After 9/11

Although there is considerable evidence suggesting that the majority of Muslim Americans hold similar mainstream religious, political, and family values, customs, and beliefs to non-Muslims, Muslim Americans continue to serve as the primary targets of the U.S. post-9/11 war on terror (Gaskew 2008). LeMay (2005) has argued that after the 9/11 incident Muslims in the United States have faced discrimination and oppression comparable to the one meted out to the Japanese Americans during the Second World War. CAIR (2005) estimates that around 1,200 Muslims in the United States were detained in a few months by the police in the aftermath of 9/11 attack. Cole (2003: 25) conservatively estimates that domestic detentions of Muslim Americans have surpassed 5,000. Gaskew (2008) suggests that in 2007 the number of civil rights complaints against the police in the United States touched a figure of 2,652. Most of the discriminatory practices in screening of passengers in air travel stems from the provisions of the Patriot Act.

The Pew Research Center (2007) has reported that 74% of Muslim Americans believe the U.S.'s anti-terrorism policies single them out for increased surveillance and monitoring. Nearly half (45%) of non-Muslims surveyed believe anti-terrorism policies target Muslim Americans and just over half overall (52%) indicated they were bothered by these policies. The majority (63%) of the Muslim Americans surveyed felt that Americans are generally intolerant of Muslims; 57% stated they knew of either family or friends who had experienced anti-Muslim discrimination. The overwhelming majority (89%) of all Muslim Americans surveyed believed anti-Muslim discrimination was primarily displayed in terms of the hostility, distrust, racial profiling, and harassment perpetrated by law enforcement agencies around the country, and that the U.S. government is actually fighting a war against Islam instead of against terrorism.

Gaskew (2008: 103) reports that all of his research subjects perceived the events of 9/11 as a "significant crossroads for their lives." These attacks triggered an internal dialogue among Muslims forcing them to take a self-critical and introspective look at their own tradition and system of beliefs within the practice of Islam and the use of violence. This has become a critical period for the development of another Islamic identity as Muslims begin to understand how the events of September 11, 2001 are shaping the perception of other communities and affecting their future in this country. Elliot (2005) reports that Muslims perceive a serious increase in bias crimes against them. Citing a study conducted by the Council on American-Islamic Relations [CAIR], an Islamic advocacy group in Washington, D.C. the report found more than 1,500 cases of harassment and anti-Muslim violence around the country in 2004, including 141 hate crimes, compared with 1,019 cases and 93 hate crimes in 2003. A study conducted by Vera institute between 2003 and 2005 found a growing perception of victimization, suspicion of security agencies, and concerns about their civil liberties. The Arab-Americans expressed serious concerns about racial profiling and immigration-related issues (Elliot 2006). A Pew research study (2007) also found that Muslims perceived being singled out for surveillance by the government.

The American Arab Anti-Discrimination Committee found in a survey that more than 700 violent incidents and 800 cases of employment discrimination were reported by Muslim Americans following the 9/11 attacks (Gaskew 2008). CAIR (2005) also reported a rise by more than 52% in hate crimes targeting Muslims in the United States after 2001. More disturbingly, under the U.S. Patriot Act special registration including fingerprinting, photographing, and interviewing was conducted on more than 80,000 men from predominantly Arab and Muslim countries (Cole 2003). A study by Muslims in American Public Square (2004) found 63% of the American Muslims felt that that their community is generally intolerant of them and 57% stated they knew either family or friends who have experienced anti-Muslim discrimination. Most of this discrimination was expressed in terms of hostility, racial profiling by the police, or government harassment. Gaskew (2008: 37) states, "over one third of the Muslims in America have felt that the U.S. is fighting a war against Islam instead of terrorism."

The impact of the U.S. Patriot Act on the Muslim community has been devastating. This Act increased the authority for conducting surveillance, collecting intelligence, investigating financial transactions, and strengthening the laws against terrorism (Neuburger 2005). Gaskew (2008) in his survey found that invariably all the Muslim subjects perceived the Act to be directed solely against the Muslims. Abdul, one of the participants in this survey stated that the Act was "directed to humiliate the Muslim Americans ..." and that "it is a political tool used to demonize Muslims" ... "making them the bad guy in the war on terror (Gaskew 2008: 154)." Cole (2003: xxiii) adds,

> The Arab and Muslim communities in the United States have been the targets of zero-tolerance immigration enforcement since 9/11, yet few if any terrorists have been identified and brought to justice through these efforts. Meanwhile thousands have been subjected to treatment that no one else – citizen or foreign national – has had to undergo.

The special registration program promoted by this Act has created the provision of finger-printing, photographing, and asking detailed background information from those seeking entry to the United States. An estimated 14,000 Muslims have been placed into removal proceedings based on this provision (Gaskew 2008: 159). Many respondents reported staying locked up for weeks at a time fearing being targeted for deportation. Gaskew (2008: 161) reports, "Several participants believed the U.S. Patriot Act has hurt the war on terror, creating an atmosphere of severe distrust and animosity between Muslims in the U.S. and law enforcement agencies which serve them." Furthermore, Muslims reported that a damaging impact of the Act was the destruction of the relationship between Muslims and police. They felt that the officers were targeting them and that they were victims of racial profiling. Several reports have been made about traffic stops by police officers for no reason by over-zealous police agencies. Moreover, during these traffic stops every vehicle occupant would be asked to provide proof of his or her U.S. citizenship. Qasim, a physician described how he was stopped on a major road and asked questions about his birth-place, proof of citizenship, and had to consent to search of his car. Tariq, another Muslim from Orlando was stopped when he was dropping his son at the school. While his son cried and all the children looked on he was questioned about his citizenship and had to step out of the car while being questioned. Zayd was stopped for speeding and the officers asked his wife, sitting beside him to take off her niqaab (all cited in Gaskew 2008). It appeared that police officers would deliberately humiliate the Muslims in the aftermath of September 11 attacks. CAIR (2005) cites several complaints of aggressive tactics used by the police officers including threats of deportation to force the Muslims into becoming police informants. The Patriot Act has deepened "the feelings of shame, guilt and humiliation emanating from the 'government supported' Islamophobic social environment" (Gaskew 2008: 170). The community has viewed even some routine practices with suspicion. The NYPD monitors everyone in the city who changes his or her name. The *Dawn* (2011), a prominent newspaper from Pakistan reported that for those whose names sound Arabic or might be from Muslim countries, police run comprehensive background checks that include reviewing travel records, criminal histories, business licenses, and immigration documents. Furthermore, the report adds that the FBI has its own ethnic mapping program that singled out Muslim communities and targeted mosques. All these reports serve to draw attention to the discrimination and victimization of Muslims in the United States.

Muslims in Europe

There are an estimated 15–20 million Muslims in Europe and their numbers are expected to double by 2025. In Europe, Islam is the second largest religion after Christianity. In large parts of the Balkans and Eastern Europe Muslims have been living for centuries. In Western Europe, the majority of Muslims are migrants and their offspring are from predominantly Muslim countries. These migrants were either recruited in the 1960s and 1970s as guest workers from the Mediterranean (Turkey and Morocco) or were part of the large post-colonial migration waves (i.e., Pakistan, Algeria, and Surinam). Following family reunifications, large Muslim communities started to emerge from the second half of the 1970s onwards. In the 1980s their descendants (the second generation of Muslim youth raised in Western Europe) entered the education system and the labor market. At present new inflows of Muslims to Western Europe are predominantly political asylum seekers from Muslim countries such as Iraq or Afghanistan. The share of Muslims in the population of Western European countries is highest in France, followed by The Netherlands, Denmark, Switzerland, and Germany (cited in *Forum* 2008).

The following table provides broad frequency counts for the Muslims in Europe: Approx % share of Muslims in various Western European countries

France	Holland	Denmark	Switzerland	Belgium	Germany	UK	Spain	Italy
6.4– 9.6%	5.8%	2.8–5.0%	4.2%	3.8–4.0%	3.6–4.2%	2.8%	0.9–2.3%	1.4%

These figures are compiled from the different national statistical agencies. As no country has statistics of the religious faiths adhered by their citizens, these figures are mostly estimates based on samples (cited in *Forum* 2008)

Most of the Muslims live in capital cities or industrial towns and have become an integral and long-standing fabric of their communities. In a study of 11 E.U. cities by the Open Society Institute (2010) it was seen that Muslims are more attached to their neighborhoods and local communities for which they had stronger feelings than for the nation. But cultural identification increased with integration in other areas such as employment and education. The OSI report also found that there is greater interaction among people of different backgrounds mostly occurring at work, school, public spaces, and shopping arenas. Surprisingly, Muslim women born in Europe had significant contact outside the home with people of other backgrounds. Interestingly, contrary to general belief, Muslims preferred living in mixed neighborhoods and furthermore, Muslims are also increasingly standing for political office though they face additional scrutiny and questions because of their background and religious beliefs. These observations suggest that Muslims have become an integral part of the European milieu.

Situation of Muslims in Europe

Unfortunately, the overall situation in Europe is not much different than the one seen in the United States. It has been reported that "the broad picture confirms that Muslims as a whole occupy an underprivileged position" in England and Wales (Peach 2005: 29). More specifically, Muslims of Pakistani and Bangladeshi descent occupy one of the poorest, if not *the* poorest, ethnic economic positions in British society (Anwar 2005; Peach 2005). Muslim men in particular are viewed as "troublesome" and prone to violence. Most anti-terrorist measures and counter-terrorism surveillance by the police appear to be directed at them. There was also the perception about "a certain level of acceptance that Islamophobic instances are the norm rather than the exception, a part of individuals' [Muslims] everyday lives" (Spalek et al. 2008: 10). Moreover, "Hard" policing approaches, including increased stop and search, nonconviction and high-profile raids, and the perception of an increase in aggressive attempts at recruiting informers are creating barriers to good police–community relations, and subsequent partnership. This has helped "create a sense of grievance amongst Muslims, with individuals arguing that they feel that they are suspect communities" (Spalek et al. 2008: 9).

In the Netherlands today, Muslim communities are – rightly or wrongly – associated with tensions, violence, and radicalization, which is a new perception escalating after 9/11. Veldhuis and Bakker (2009: 8) argue that radical Islamism has been generally regarded as a threat to the state, Dutch society, and Muslim immigrant communities in general. The Dutch perception has grown that "Muslims respond violently to any political incident that speaks against their culture" (Veldhuis and Bakker 2009: 3). This has a long history in the country and the first signs of radicalization date back to the 1980s. Muslim individuals and groups started to organize themselves around issues such as the start of the first Palestinian intifada in 1987, and the row over Salman Rushdie's *Satanic Verses* in 1988. This intensified particularly after the assassination of Theo van Gogh, who was murdered by a radical Islamist named Mohammed Bouyeri. Radicalization of Muslim youth received "extensive attention by Dutch media, policy-makers, politicians and academics" (Veldhuis and Bakker 2009: 4–5). After the attacks on the United States on September 11, 2001, the idea that "Muslims posed a threat to Dutch society – even to the extent of considering them a Trojan horse or a fifth column" – began to gain ground (Veldhuis and Bakker 2009: 11).

According to a survey of attitudes towards Muslims in 11 cities of Europe (Open Society Institute 2010) there is evidence that apart from the general anti-immigrant bias there is also a specific anti-Muslim prejudice that has developed out of a stereotype-generating process in the last few decades. Muslim respondents, particularly the women, also perceived higher levels of religious discrimination than non-Muslims in the 11 cities. The Muslims also have an uneasy relationship with the police across continental Europe. Since 9/11 the community has faced increased police surveillance and experienced an increase in hate and violent crimes. There is also a growing anxiety and disinclination towards a multicultural society. A quarter of respondents were "resistant" to a mixed society and felt their cities have reached a limit in this regard.

Many incidents have triggered these responses and perceptions of Muslims as violent people. For example, in The Netherlands on October 2007, Bilal Bajaka, a young Dutch Muslim of Moroccan descent, entered a police station in Amsterdam, pulled a knife and stabbed two police officers. In self-defense, one of the officers shot the man who died on the spot. Immediately, the incident prompted questions about the perpetrator's motivations. Bajaka was probably not radicalized and apparently, he was a suicidal schizophrenic who had just left a psychiatric clinic where he had been treated for mental problems. Nevertheless, especially after it turned out that in 2005, Bajaka had loose contacts with some of the members of the Hofstadgroep, the radical network that included the murderer of filmmaker

Theo van Gogh, the media started speculating about whether Bajaka was a radical Islamist and whether the Netherlands was the target of a terrorist attack. Although the Bajaka case was unrelated to radicalization or terrorism, the incident triggered riots among young Muslims in immigrant neighborhoods in Amsterdam and fueled tensions between Muslim and non-Muslim communities in the Netherlands (Veldhuis and Bakker 2009: 4). General perception of radicalization among Muslim youth was heightened after the murder of Theo van Gogh even though it was a rare event. Tajfel and Turner (1979: 6) state that "irrespective of the presence of competition or conflicting group interests, the mere act of categorizing individuals into groups can generate tensions and conflicts between groups." Consequently, many young, second-generation Muslims in the West face an identity crisis (Choudhury 2007; Malik 2007). They face a generational conflict with their parents. On the other hand, they do not feel fully accepted by Dutch society. Buijs, Demant, and Hamdy (2006), for example, suggest that Moroccan youngsters in The Netherlands feel alienated from both their parents and Dutch society and have a hybrid-identity that is not recognized and accepted by their direct environment. Consequently, they find a satisfactory identity in the *Ummah* that connects them with other Muslims and for which nationality, be it Moroccan or Dutch, becomes irrelevant.

Veldhuis and Bakker (2009: 8) state,

radicalization among Muslims in the Netherlands is not a post-9/11 phenomenon. However, since the attacks on the United States in 2001, this process and in particular radical Islamism has been generally regarded as a threat to the state, Dutch society and Muslim immigrant communities in general. This feeling was intensified by a series of terrorist incidents and numerous scandals in the Netherlands that revealed extremist, discriminatory and illegal practices by a number of radical Islamist groups and institutions.

An early study by Erasmus University of Rotterdam in 1994 (cited in Veldhuis and Bakker 2009), found that radical Islamists had attempted to impede the process of integration of Muslims in Dutch society but had not been very successful in their endeavor. Furthermore, it concluded that very few Muslims wanted to challenge existing social structures in The Netherlands. However, various terrorist attacks by Islamists, including those in France (attacks by the Algerian Groupe Islamique Armé), Israel (suicide attacks on buses in Jerusalem), and the United States (the 1993 attack on the World Trade Center), were some factors that generated negative stereotypes of Muslims in Europe and promoted prejudices toward Islam.

After the attacks on the United States on September 11, 2001, the idea that Muslims were dangerous to Dutch society was gaining ground. This perception was bolstered by reports about the deaths at the hands of Indian security forces in Kashmir of two Dutch citizens of Moroccan descent who were believed to be jihadists. The boys who died in December 2001 shortly after their arrival in the troubled Indian territory were associated with one of the most radical mosques in the Netherlands, the Al-Fourqaan mosque in the city of Eindhoven (Veldhuis and Bakker 2009: 11). The murder of Theo van Gogh in 2004 was a significant event that inflamed intercultural and interethnic tensions between different social groups and led on some occasions, to violent outbursts in many parts of Europe. Such incidents also contributed to political polarization over issues related to Muslims and their practice of Islam. Unfortunately, these have further reinforced the views that Muslims are prone to violence.

The situation in the United Kingdom is perhaps even more disturbing. The discourse on "terrorism" has been led by the construction of Muslim minorities as comprising communities who are at risk from violent extremism. Young Muslim men in particular have been viewed as constituting a "problem group" and have become the predominant targets of anti-terrorist legislation and counter-terrorism surveillance policing in Britain (Poynting and Mason 2006) and other countries. A report (Spalek et al. 2008: 9) cites a Muslim stating that "they do not understand Islam and the Muslim communities and everybody is tarnished by the same brush." This report describes the various ways in which the Muslim communities have experienced "hard policing" and its ill consequences. These approaches have included increased stop and search, nonconviction and high profile raids, and the perception of an increase in aggressive attempts at recruiting informers. Muslim community leaders have pointed out that such practices are creating barriers to good police–community relations, and a sense of grievance among the Muslims. Such suspicion is having grave consequences upon the individuals and their families causing job losses, family breakdown, mental health issues, and even ostracism from their wider communities. Moreover individuals on the receiving end of "hard" tactics were often too frightened to report incidents even to community groups. Individuals described how they were pressured to explain the construction of their Muslim identities, particularly in relation to "Britishness."

Moreover, like the United States, the British government too enacted a new law called the Anti Terrorism, Crime, and Security Act 2001. This Act has introduced a religiously aggravated element to crime, which involves imposing higher penalties upon offenders who are motivated by religious hatred. Spalek, Awa and McDonald (2008) report that the perception was that it was the Islamic faith that was being targeted. Islamophobia was a significant issue for the individuals who were interviewed by these authors. Instances of Islamophobia that interviewees referred to included verbal and physical abuse, threats, physical assaults, and homes and cars being firebombed or with acids. Unfortunately, the reporting of instances of Islamophobia was rare for most participants in the survey did not want to create a fuss around their experiences. Esposito and Mogahed (2007: 1) state, "When the Western media talks about Islam and Muslim culture, discussion tends to center on religious extremism and global terrorism."

Police Attempts to Reach Out to Muslim Community

The police forces in all these nations have realized the importance of building trust with the Muslim community and engaging them directly. Gaskew (2008: 182) states, "the law enforcement agencies are obligated to do everything in their power, morally, ethically, and tactically to create an environment conducive to obtaining cooperation from Muslim [American] citizens and maintaining an active channel of human intelligence." Most police departments are attempting to act proactively in reaching out to the Muslim residents and while their focus remains on counter-terrorism, their efforts involve understanding, dialogue, and participation.

The police are beginning to take steps in learning about the history, tradition, values, and practices of Muslim communities and particularly about what are sensitive issues for the people. As Gaskew (2008) advocates, the officers need to understand the religion of Islam and this requires a good understanding of major Islamic texts and principles such as Qur'an, Hadith, and Shariah. Many police units such as at Chicago (Ramirez et al. 2005a) have begun "cultural diversity" training for their personnel and part of this training is to understand that not all Muslims share similar cultural traits. Based on their race, ethnicity, and national identity Muslims follow a diverse range of practices. The best way to build such an understanding is to enter into a dialogue with the community members. Dawoud, a Pakistani–American stated to Gaskew (2008: 186), "Dialogue is the primary instrument of communication … police must make a concerted effort at establishing a proactive dialogue that focuses upon mutual interests …. And problems of the community … Muslims must also benefit from this dialogue." Finally, the police have displayed the need to participate in community activities to strengthen their bonds and help remove misgivings about their functions. Such interaction with the police has likely led to Muslims taking a self-critical analysis of their faith and confronting those who advocate extremism.

In the 11 European cities studied by the Open Society Institute (2010) several innovative examples have emerged that seek to increase the partnership of Muslims in community-led initiatives with the local police forces. The Netherlands have started a publicly funded "Neighborhood Fathers" project that engages Moroccan fathers concerned about the confrontation of police with the young men from their community. These people have started patrolling their streets to prevent trouble and provide an interface with the police authorities. In Leicester, United Kingdom, a Police Advisory Group on Racial Incidents has been set up to advise senior officers on critical incidents. Members meet to discuss hypothetical situations that may turn ugly and discuss how community involvement can mitigate them. Community groups have even come forward to work with the police and support their counter-terrorism efforts. In London, a Youth Independent Advisory Group has held training sessions with police recruits to devise unobtrusive stop and search operations, particularly with minority groups keeping in mind their cultural sensitivities.

The police have also started working directly with mosques in many communities. The Amsterdam police engaged the mosque to share information about their actions when a Moroccan youth was killed when attacking the officers with a knife. "The release of the anti-Islam movie 'Fitna' by the Dutch Member of Parliament Geert Wilders, early 2008, aroused anxious fears of angry responses by Muslims communities" (Veldhuis and Bakker 2009: 1). In 2004, Muslims in The Netherlands [and around the world] had reacted violently to the publication of a Danish cartoon, which led to the murder of Theo van Gogh. Similar apprehension was expressed about this movie that it will trigger violent demonstrations, boycotts, the burning of flags, and other aggressive responses by Muslim communities, both in the

Netherlands and around the world. Even the Dutch Prime Minister publicly expressed his concerns and consequences for Muslim integration in Dutch society.

However, the police in Amsterdam and Rotterdam closely cooperated with the local Muslim communities to reduce tensions. The police organized community meetings to explain the legal position in filing complaints about the film. These efforts helped and there were no noticeable incidents at all. Eloquent young Muslims stepped forward as representatives for their communities and of Islam, explicitly distancing themselves from radical or violent action by Muslims in answer to the film. Likewise, orthodox Muslims made strong pleas to react in a nonviolent and dignified way to *Fitna*.

The German police in Berlin have built regular contacts with the Muslims through the development of "cooperation agreements." This involves a program called Transfer of Intercultural agreements that helps bring the police and mosque authorities together to provide the police with information about Islam and culture of Muslim communities. These are helping prevent conflicts between the community and the official authorities over misunderstanding and misinformation (Open Society Institute 2010).

Community-oriented policing in particular has been helpful in seeking the cooperation of Muslim communities. In The Netherlands, "neighborhood directors" and "street coaches" visit individuals at home and talk to their parents as part of a movement led by the police. Many representatives from the minority Muslim groups have been recruited for these tasks to work from within the community. Many community-oriented policing programs have begun to focus upon the problems of Muslim minorities and to include them in local security efforts.

Furthermore, police departments across Europe are opening the organization to recruit members of minority communities. In Rotterdam, 60 internships have been offered to future police officers that are targeted at non-native students (Open Society Institute 2010: 185). Police are now advertising vacancies through posters pasted on mosque bulletin boards that carry photographs of Muslim police officers. Unfortunately, Islamophobia and racism persists in police unions and in Amsterdam almost a fifth of Muslim police officers were contemplating leaving the force due to discrimination. Nevertheless, most police forces are developing imaginative initiatives to engage the Muslim community and build trust in their organization.

In the United Kingdom, the police have engaged with the Muslim communities in a multilayered format. Different cross-sections of police from the local level ranging from community liaison to counter-terrorism officers to national units such as the National Communities Tension Team [NCTT] have been interacting with the Muslims. This NCTT is a central policing unit working with all forces to monitor intercommunity and intracommunity tensions nationwide. "There is also diversity in relation to the different parts of Muslim communities with whom engagement takes place, from grassroots youth groups, to various national representative bodies and religious institutions" (Spalek et al. 2008: 11). The London metropolitan police established a new unit called the Muslim Contact Unit as also a Strategic Contact Unit after the 9/11 incident to engage and work with the Muslims. This operated under the tradition of community policing and sought to build trust among the

Muslims. The objectives were to build specialist knowledge about the community and bring back those who had been marginalized and alienated. A clear aim was also to involve the community in gathering intelligence and spotting radicals formenting trouble in the community. Yet, the efforts were made through negotiation and engagement with the community.

Another issue that has been stressed is to provide reassurance policing in the context of racial and Islamophobic attacks on the Muslims. It has been observed that Muslim police officers working in such units brought with them not only "operational policing and community policing experience, but also social and cultural capital that may enable them to build partnerships with particular minorities of the Muslim population" (Spalek et al. 2008: 12). Such a "hard/soft" policing approach helped in gaining the adherence of the community and their support in counter terrorism work too.

Another successful strategy adopted by the British police is the so-called "neighborhood policing" (Innes 2006). The police have established strategic contacts with community elders and opinion formers to develop a "community intelligence feed" about the activities of individuals and groups in these communities of interest to the police as also to counteract rumors or other information. Significantly, neighborhood police officers have also been tasked to develop the key collective problems affecting local security. After several local problems have been identified then all local people are given an opportunity to vote on their priorities for police action at specially convened police and community meetings. The importance of this policy is that "this process amounts to constructing a knowledge base about the drivers of insecurity in the neighborhoods where officers are working and providing the opportunity for local people to democratically influence how they are policed" (Innes 2006: 235). This is a healthy departure for the common forms of policing have always been to either "over police" the minorities as suspects or "under-policed" as victims (Bowling 1999). This policy has made the police more responsive to community concerns and in return has enabled the officers to persuade the community members of the benefits to work with the police. "The particular advantages of NP are that it provides local communities with a degree of collective influence over how they are policed and that in acting to address locally defined problems, neighborhood officers are well placed to generate trust and collect community intelligence" (Innes 2006: 239).

Another issue that was stressed by the U.K. police was to stress the knowledge of Islam for their officers. A research finding substantiated that "Religious knowledge is essential in fighting violent ideology, both with regards to understanding and developing counter arguments for the motivations of individuals and groups supporting and using violence, and also in the motivations of those seeking to prevent violence from an Islamic paradigm" (Spalek et al. 2008: 16). Belief and faith in the religion play an important role in building closer contact with the community and those with strong religious motivations surprisingly co-operated more with the police to counter the violent ideology perpetuated in the name of their religion. Regular communication and openness in accepting differences were essential in generating an honest dialogue and marginalizing those who argued for a unitary interpretation of Islam. The police have also been working with women and youth and have found them to be most productive in gaining allegiance of the community.

Policing Muslims in the United States After 9/11

Since 9/11, both federal and local law enforcement have initiated outreach efforts to Muslim communities in the United States. The Homeland Security Institute (2006) study suggests that police efforts in building partnerships appear to be strongest in those areas where the Muslim community is highly concentrated geographically, cohesive, and has long-standing political and social organizations. Furthermore, once outreach efforts were initiated critical success came from selecting the right law enforcement representatives and empowering them suitably. The police also sought to prioritize initiatives based on mutual objectives, providing a rapid response to community concerns, and developing a joint approach for interfacing with the media. The Chicago police department's multicultural forum has been fairly successful in working with the minorities (Ramirez et al. 2005a). The police sought "relationship-building leaders" on both the sides and took the lead in reaching out to key community leaders. The officers assigned to the community outreach programs avoided focusing on contacts solely for information extraction and instead focused upon information sharing. A special effort was made to identify community leaders who were genuinely representative of the diverse groups within the Muslim community and the police organized periodic formal as well as informal meetings to share each others' concerns. The Chicago Police Department has further gained trust by their willingness to explain, to the extent possible, the rationale behind actions that affect the communities and by their rapid response to community needs.

The St. Paul police also designed a customized community-policing program to reach the Muslims of their region (Ramirez et al. 2004). The community is largely from East Africa and consists of various national and ethnic groups. Accordingly, the police adopted individualized efforts with multiple venues to conduct outreach on a broader scale. Before initiating a dialogue with the communities, local law enforcement interviewed individuals to identify who the formal and informal community leaders were. The police realized that instead of imams, community elders held leadership positions in everyday life and were the key to building trust with the members. The elders' assistance was crucial in addressing concerns whenever an incident involving some community member occurred.

As part of its Partnering for Prevention and Community Safety Initiative, Northeastern University developed a "Promising Practices Guide" that outlines promising practices for building relationships among federal, state, and local law enforcement and the American Muslim, Arab, and Sikh communities in order to enhance counter-terrorism initiatives, protect the community from hate crimes and hate incidents, and preserve civil rights (Ramirez et al. 2004). The Partnering for Prevention group conducted a number of case studies in communities that attempted partnerships and developed a framework for evaluating them and factors that appear to be critical to success. This study pointed out that after 9/11, local law enforcement and the Arab and Muslim community in Dearborn, Michigan and the Greater Detroit area forged a highly successful, collaborative relationship. The study suggested that the Muslim community itself was very proactive in cooperating with the police that demonstrated remarkable flexibility and brought innovative problem solving to enhance the effectiveness of the partnership. The police also backed up their words with action and responded swiftly to concerns within the community and worked rapidly to address issues that threatened to damage the trust they had built with community leaders. Both the community and law enforcement demonstrated an early understanding of the importance of public statements and utilized the media to clarify positions and to debunk myths and stereotypes. In many cases, community and law enforcement held joint press conferences, to defuse misinformation and build trust with the broader community.

In Washington, D.C. area that is home to a large Arab American population the community leaders themselves formed an Advisory Council that became the mechanism for facilitating a partnership between a number of diverse communities and associations and federal law enforcement. The FBI served as a focal point of law enforcement efforts and explained ongoing terrorist initiatives to the group, helping to dispel misapprehensions (Ramirez et al. 2005b).

Conclusion

The partnership between the Muslim community and the police is important and significant. Yet, the continuing terrorist attacks and troubles in the Middle East and Afghanistan–Pakistan region suggest that terrorism will "continue to influence the lens through which many in government and academia view the world's Muslims" (Silk 2010: 212). This is unfortunate for the Muslims will also continue to perceive that law enforcement personnel and government are biased towards them. This partnership is dependent upon the relationship built between police personnel and individuals within the Muslim community. Consequently, it is necessary that both the police and the community pay attention to the need for relationships, learning, negotiation, and flexibility when working in the continuing hostile environment. Senior police officers and community elders stressed the need of joint police and Muslim community efforts to defeat terrorism. The U.K. Government's "CONTEST" counter-terrorism strategy has further emphasized the importance of partnerships between Muslims and police, particularly in the "Prevent" strand of the agenda (HM Government 2009).

However, many precautions are needed in constructing this partnership. While the police priority remains in gathering intelligence for counter-terrorism objectives the Muslim communities may be wary of such queries from officers with whom they have not developed a trusting relationship. This requires considerable interpersonal skills, patience, and understanding on the part of the police officers who need to tread cautiously. There are various personal ways in which police officers and Muslims could connect as they seek to work together. Silk's (2010: 197) interviewees fondly spoke of "visits by a police leader to mosques during *Eid*, officers talking about family with community members and avoiding inappropriate questions about terrorism, a 'gem of a police officer' who would have tea and some laughs with kids at a youth center, and the value of getting to know officers by their first names." Spalek, Awa, and McDonald (2009) also narrate about an officer who visits a Muslim community member in a hospital while off duty and the impact such gestures can have in building trust with the community.

Yet, it is not enough to build personal rapport. Police officers must strive to learn about the Muslim community and make efforts to understand their religion. Esposito and Mogahed (2007: xiii) stress, "Muslims around the world say that the one thing the West can do to improve relations with their societies is to moderate their views and respect Islam." Religion remains an important and integral part of Muslim identity. The police officers working with the community cannot be effective unless they begin to understand the beliefs, rituals, and cultural practices that form part of the religion.

Furthermore, most police efforts are hampered by organizational limitations. Ramirez, O'Connell, and Zafar (2005a) found in their study of Chicago police that a key drawback in developing a sustained partnership with the Muslim community was the high level of personnel turnover, particularly on the part of law enforcement, given the importance of personal relationships. Another shortcoming was the lack of sufficient authority at the low-level ranks to make decisions that will affect the community. It is also important for the police to engage all the sections of the community for there is the possibility that the police may get embroiled in internal disputes of the community and antagonize some members.

Above all, it has to be recognized that police alone cannot build a partnership with the estranged Muslim community. Other state institutions and groups need to play their part in giving a sense of equality and acceptance to the Muslims in order to integrate them amicably in western societies. The Muslims also have to play a proactive role in correcting prejudice and negative stereotypes directed against them. They have to raise their voice against those who seek to radicalize their young members and thrust a unitary interpretation of the religion. Ultimately, every citizen and community groups have to initiate actions and make efforts to bring changes in policies that cause discrimination and inequalities that lead to oppression and alienation.

References

Abbas, T. (2007). Muslim minorities in Britain: Integration, multiculturalism, and racism in the post-7/7 period'. *Journal of Intercultural Studies, 28*(3), 287–300.

Ahmed, A. S. (1993). *Discovering Islam: Making sense of Muslim history and society*. New York: Routledge.

Anwar, M. (2005). Issues, policy, and practice. In T. Abbas (Ed.), *Muslim Britain: Communities under pressure* (pp. 31–46). London: Zed Books.

Bowling, B. (1999). *Violent racism: Victimization, policing and social control*. Oxford: Clarendon.

Buijs, F., Demant, F., & Hamdy, A. (2006). *Strijders van eigen bodem. Radicale en democratische moslims in Nederland* (Worriers of own soil. Radical and democratic Muslims in the Netherlands). Amsterdam: Amsterdam University Press.

Cainkar, L. (2002). No longer visible: Arab and Muslim exclusion after September 11. *Middle East Report, 224*, 22–29.

Canefe, N. (2008). Religion and politics in the Diaspora: The case of Canadian Muslims. *Journal of Community and Applied Social Psychology, 18*(4), 390–394.

Choudhury, T. (2007). *The role of Muslim identity politics in radicalisation (a study in progress).* Department for Communities and Local Government, London.

Cole, D. (2003). *Enemy aliens: Double standards and constitutional freedom in the war on terrorism.* New York: The New York Press.

Council on American Islamic Relations [CAIR]. (2005). *The status of Muslim civil rights in the United States: Unequal protection.* Washington, DC: CAIR Publication.

Dawn. (2011). *NYPD shadows Muslims who change names.* 26 October.

Elliot, A. (2005). *Muslims report 50% increase in bias crimes.* New York Times, 12 May 2005.

Elliot, A. (2006). *After 9/11, Arab-Americans fear police acts, study finds.* New York Times, 12 July 2006.

Esposito, J. L., & Mogahed, D. (2007). *Who speaks for Islam: What a billion Muslims really think.* New York: Gallup Press.

Forum. (2008). *The position of Muslims in The Netherlands: Facts and figures.* Utrecht: FORUM, Institute for Multicultural Development.

Gaskew, T. (2008). *Policing Muslim American communities: A compendium of post 9/11 interviews.* Lewiston: Edwin Mellen Press.

Haddad, Y. Y. (2004). *Not quite American: The shaping of Arab and Muslim identity in the United States.* Waco: Baylor University Press.

Haddad, Y. Y., & Lummis, A. (1987). *Islamic values in the United States: A comparative study.* New York: Oxford University Press.

Hasisi, B. (2008). Police, politics and culture in deeply divided society. *The Journal of Criminal Law and Criminology, 98*(3), 1119–1145.

HM Government. (2009). *Pursue prevent protect prepare: The United Kingdom's strategy for countering international terrorism.* Norwich: TSO. Retrieved from http://www.official-documents.gov.uk/document/cm75/7547/7547.pdf.

Homeland Security Institute. (2006). *Community policing within Muslim communities: An overview and annotated bibliography of open- source literature.* Arlington: Homeland Security Institute, HSI Publication Number: RP06-99-01.

Innes, M. (2006). Policing uncertainty: Countering terror through community intelligence and democratic policing. *The Annals of the American Academy of Political and Social Science, 605*, 222–241.

Khan, K. (2009). *Preventing violent extremism (PVE) and PREVENT: A response from the Muslim community.* London: An-Nisa Society. Retrieved from http://www.an-nisa.org/downloads/PVE_&_Prevent_-__A_Muslim_response.pdf.

LeMay, M. (2005). *The perennial struggle: Race, ethnicity and minority group relations in the United States* (2nd ed.). Upper Saddle River: Prentice Hall.

Leonard, K. (2002). South Asian leadership of American Muslims. In Y. Y. Haddad (Ed.), *Muslims in the West: From sojourners to citizens.* Oxford: Oxford University Press.

Malik, S. (2007). 'My brother the bomber'. *Prospect Magazine*, 31 May 2007.

Muslims in the American public Square: Shifting political winds and fallout from 9/11, Afghanistan and Iraq. (2004). Project MAPS: Muslims in American public square, Georgetown University's center for Muslim-Christian understanding. Washington, DC: Georgetown University Publications.

Neuburger, D. W. (2005). *America's courts and the criminal justice system* (8th ed.). Belmont: Thompson/Wadsworth.

Nimer, M. (2002). Muslims in American public life. In Y. Y. Haddad (Ed.), *Muslims in the West: From sojourners to citizens.* Oxford: Oxford University Press.

Open Society Institute. (2010). *Muslims in Europe: A report on 11 EU cities*. London: Open Society Foundation.

Peach, C. (2005). Britain's Muslim population: An overview. In T. Abbas (Ed.), *Muslim Britain: Communities under pressure* (pp. 18–30). London: Zed Books.

Pew Research Center. (2007). *Muslim Americans: Middle class and mostly mainstream*. Retrieved from http://pewresearch.org/assets/pdf/muslim-americans.pdf.

Pew Survey. (2009). *Mapping the global Muslim population: A report on the size and distribution of the world's Muslim population*. October 2009.

Poynting, S., & Mason, V. (2006). Tolerance, freedom, justice and peace: Britain, Australia and anti-Muslim racism since 11th September 2001. *Journal of Intercultural Studies, 27*(4), 365–392.

Ramirez, D. A., O'Connell, S. C., & Zafar, R. (2004). *Developing partnerships between law enforcement and American Muslim, Arab and Sikh communities: A promising practices guide*. Boston: Northeastern University.

Ramirez, D. A., O'Connell, S. C., & Zafar, R. (2005a). *Developing partnerships between law enforcement and American Muslim, Arab and Sikh communities: The greater Chicago experience*. Boston: Northeastern University.

Ramirez, D., O'Connell, S. C., & Zafar, R. (2005b). *Developing partnerships between law enforcement and American Muslim, Arab and Sikh communities: The Washington, DC experience*. Boston: Northeastern University.

Silk, P. D. (2010). *Planning outreach between Muslim communities and police in the USA and the UK*. Doctoral Thesis, The University of Georgia, Athens.

Spalek, B., El Awa, S., & McDonald, L. Z. (2008). *Police-Muslim engagement for the purpose of counter-terrorism: An examination*. Birmingham: The University of Birmingham.

Tajfel, H., & Turner, J. (1979). An integrative theory of intergroup conflict. In W. G. Austin & S. Worchel (Eds.), *The social psychology of intergroup relations* (pp. 33–47). Monterey: Brooks-Cole.

Tyler, T. R. (2005). Policing in black and white: Ethnic group differences in trust and confidence in the police. *Police Quarterly, 8*, 322.

Veldhuis, T., & Bakker, E. (2009). Muslims in The Netherlands: Tensions and violent conflict, MICROCON Policy Working Paper 6, Brighton, MICROCON.

Chapter 4
Human Rights and Islamic Law

Sharia and the Distribution of Power

The Sharia addresses the issue of the distribution of power by setting out a system that makes the state accountable for the exercise of authority based on values and norms of Muslim societies. Justice and responsibility are connected to views regarding the nature of power. According to the Muslim view, power is based on an extremely wide range of sources. Some of these could be one's rhetorical abilities and wealth. Because power is diverse and very difficult to hold on to, others may increasingly challenge the status quo from diverse bases (Rosen 2000). In order to safeguard the individual from the arbitrary use of power by the state, the sharia sets up a system to manage and control the use of political power. Accordingly, rights imply obligations that the state has to adhere to in its exercise of political power. Though words such as Haqq/Huquq are often translated as rights, its implications are not the same when compared to the Western idea of rights. Under the Islamic conception, Haqq (rights) also imply obligations, and more specifically the distribution of the bonds of indebtedness that exist between sentient human beings in society.

In order to give substance to the above conception, Islamic law is organized vertically, and not horizontally. Accordingly, its referent is not to the other doctrinal propositions that are logically related to one another but rather, they are arranged to form a coherent body in such a manner that the relationship between general propositions and local circumstances gives them meaning and content. From this structural perspective, the system of Islamic law is highly organized and developed. This system can be very effective in rural as well as urban areas if it is composed of two vital components. First, that the primary goal of the law is not merely to resolve differences, but rather, to restore people back to positions from where they can continue to negotiate their own arrangements, with the least amount of adverse implications for the social order. Second, even though the particular content of a court's knowledge regarding particular individuals may be both limited and stereotypical the terms or concepts employed by the courts, the styles of speech shaping testimony,

F.B. Hakeem et al., *Policing Muslim Communities: Comparative International Context*, 41
DOI 10.1007/978-1-4614-3552-5_4, © Springer Science+Business Media New York 2012

and the remedial forms that are applied are very similar to those that people use in everyday lives and have little of the strange formality or professionalized distortions of other systems of law. In Africa and the Far East the idea of law as an abstract principle is rejected. Disputes and crimes are regarded as diseases that disturb the proper functioning of the social body. When conflicts arise, they do not call for authoritarian solutions; instead, these are not only resolved, but also dissolved by conciliation procedures. The main goal in all circumstances is to restore harmony (David 1975).

Even though few comparative lawyers/professionals appreciate the fact that law is a part of culture rather than a separable and refined essence of it, not much advantage has been taken of the social science understanding regarding ideology, the role of elites, or of law as an instrument of political order.

This perspective focuses on two criteria for the purposes of legal classification. It examines the role that law plays in the overall distribution of power within society and the polity at large. Furthermore, it also focuses on the fundamentally unstable and indeterminate cultural conceptualizations that have to be considered by the legal system.

Law is a mechanism through which the values and norms of a society are articulated and given legitimate support. As such, irrespective of how it is defined, law is undeniably a part of the equation of power that is at work in the community. The key issue here is not whether power is the crucial aspect of the type of legal system at work, or a function of the enforcement apparatus of a sovereign, but rather, how the distribution of power operates via the law in ways that are deeply intermeshed with the overall distribution of power within a given society. Constitutions, codes, precedents, and others are specific means of addressing the issues of power and culture. However, these are second-order mechanisms that mediate primary factors such as how power itself is distributed and how culture is dealt with by the law.

Common law systems address both these criteria in a unique manner. Power is dispensed to the local level through different mechanisms of indirect control, while still retaining ultimate power at the top. The second issue is addressed by letting local cultural conceptualizations and information fill up most of the content of the law by indirectly administered mechanisms of incorporation.

An examination of Fig. 4.1 shows the legal system's approach to power and culture. According to this scheme the Islamic system has an open-ended culture with a moving classificatory system. It fits well into the common law system of classification. Hindu and Buddhist law have a culture that articulates concepts that are grounded in conventional behavior and follow a reciprocity-based system of law. As opposed to the above, the Confucian system is one that is absorptive and amalgamative and is amenable to legal reception. It is very similar to the civil law model. Regarding the issue of power, the Islamic system can be considered to be one that is localized, indirect, and dispersed. On the other hand, the civil law system is fairly centralized and direct. As opposed to both the above, a reciprocity-based system supports social conventions but is limited in its quest for social solutions.

According to Islamic law the political authority has an obligation not only to the people but also to God not to violate the freedom and liberties of the ruled without

Culture	System	Power	Types
Conventional behavior	Reciprocal	Limited	Hindu/Buddhist
Amalgamative	Civil	Direct	Confucian
Open-ended	Common	Indirect	Jewish/Islamic

Fig. 4.1 Legal systems approach to power/culture

justification. There is support for the justificatory principle in the Quran, where a justifying clause usually follows almost every prohibition regarding human relations.

Efforts to systematize Islamic jurisprudence were accomplished by the disciples of Muhammad bin Idris al Shafeii (d. 820), two centuries after the death of the Prophet. This accomplishment was referred to as the discipline of usul al fiqh (roots of law) and constituted the theoretical legal foundation for Islamic jurisprudence or fiqh. The two main sources of fiqh are the Quran and the Hadith. This science of usul al fiqh tries to establish a method that facilitates the Islamic legal expert (mujtahid) to make new pronouncements via ijtihad. It also enables one to extract from the indications (dalalat) in the holy texts, practical rules that furnish the best guidance to a person who is in full possession of his mental faculties and referred to via divine discourse (the Mukallaf). It covers both domains of social existence: the religious rituals (ibadat) and the more mundane social affairs (muamalat). Among the four Sunni schools of Islamic jurisprudence two other methods are recognized for inferring the law according to the sharia. These came to be recognized as ijma (consensus) and Qiyas (analogical reasoning). Under the Islamic system, the process of Ijma (consensus) is used to address issues of power. It acts as a mechanism for the distribution of power within Islamic societies. Ijma signifies agreement among Muslims in any particular age on a juridical rule. The source of authority for it is based on the following Quranic verse 4:59, surah An-Nisa (Women), which states:

"O you who believe; obey God and obey the Prophet and those of you who are in authority, and if you have a dispute concerning any matter refer it to God and the Prophet." Reference is also here made to the Hadith ascribed to the Prophet which states, "There can be no consensus on error or misguided behavior amongst my people".

Of the three types of Ijma: that of the companions of the Prophet, that of the jurists, and that of the people, the Ijma of the companions of the Prophet is universally accepted and cannot be repealed. However, this is not the case with the other two types. Ijma can be discerned explicitly or implicitly, and has equal authoritative value. In order to be valid, the Ijma has to follow certain conditions. The Ijma should not be in conflict with the Quran or the Hadith. Once a question has been determined by Ijma, it cannot be revisited by individual jurists. An earlier Ijma may be reversed by a later Ijma, and a third view is impermissible when the jurists of an era have expressed only two views on a certain question. Ijma is a valuable tool in administering Muslim societies because it helps in making changes to suit the needs of a changing society and its needs. It is influenced by the opinions of jurists in all cases where there is no guidance from the Quran or the Hadith (Johnston 2007).

An Islamic Perspective on Human Rights

Protection of human rights is a powerful tool of internationalism that pierces the sacred veil of state sovereignty for the sake of human dignity. The universality of human rights has been regularly reiterated since the adoption of the Universal Declaration of Human Rights (UDHR) by the General Assembly of the United Nations in 1948.

Many member states of the United Nations are Muslim states that apply Islamic law either wholly or in part. Furthermore, Islamic law affects in some manner, the way of life of more than a billion Muslims globally. Though many Muslim states participate in the objective of the U.N.'s human rights, many of them register their reservations and declarations based on the Sharia when ratifying international human rights treaties.

There are different perspectives regarding human rights and Islamic law. First there is a general view prevalent in the West that Islamic law is incompatible with the ideals of human rights and also that human rights cannot be obtained through the auspices of Islamic law. Alternatively, there is much pessimism in the Muslim world regarding the state of present human rights principles and the objective of the United Nations in that respect. Human rights are best protected by states from within their different domestic laws and cultures, so the relevance of Islamic law in the effective application of international human rights law in the Muslim world takes on added significance. Muslim states possess the sovereign right to apply Islamic law in their jurisdictions so the question that arises is whether international human rights can be effectively safeguarded within the confines of the application of Islamic law.

Prior studies in this area have emphasized some traditional interpretations of Islamic law and an exclusionist version of international human rights law. This has precluded the examination of many commonalities that exist between international human rights law and Islamic law and continued to advance the theory of incompatibility between them. The theory of incompatibility puts international human rights law at loggerheads with Muslim states that apply Islamic law. There are four prominent perspectives that shed light on this area of enquiry:

(a) The works of An-Na'im: *Towards an Islamic Reformation* (An-Naim 1990);
(b) Mayer's: *Islam and Human Rights* (Mayer 1999);
(c) Monshipouri's: *Islamism, Secularism, and Human Rights in the Middle East* (Monshipouri 1998);
(d) Baderin's: *International Human Rights and Islamic Law* (Baderin 2003).

According to An-Na'im, traditional Islamic law should be subjected to the jurisprudence of international human rights, by disregarding any Islamic jurisprudential justifications. He argues for an Islamic law reformation from within so as to conform to international human rights principles via a reverse process of Naskh (abrogating certain verses of the Quran by others), wherein the application of some Medinan revelations of the Quran could be abandoned in favor of other Meccan revelations. Some scholars have seriously questioned this approach as impractical (Sachedina 1993).

The main thrust of Mayer's work is that modern Islamic human rights schemes are dubious because they borrow their substance from international human rights but use Islamic law to limit human rights applications. Mayer (1999) relied mostly on the traditional interpretations of the Sharia and the practice in some Muslim countries based on those traditional interpretations, without consideration to other legally valid alternative interpretations of the Sharia in that respect. Though Mayer referred to the fact that Islamic heritage offered many humanistic values, philosophical concepts, and moral principles that were appropriately adapted towards construction of human rights principles, there was no further elaboration on these alternatives. According to Troll (1992), with regard to the crucial task of comprehensively elaborating a methodically sound and genuinely contemporary Islamic human rights teaching based on the pre-modern Islamic heritage, Mayer has been wise enough to leave these to Muslim believers and to internal doctrinal debate among them.

The main thrust of Monshipouri's work is that fusion between the secular and Islamic principles can lead to human dignity. Quraishi (2000) argues that while Monshipouri (1998) judges specific rules of Islamic law with respect to conceptual values of secularism for compatibility, he does not articulate the parallel essential values of Islam, and does not place specific secularist human rights norms against them for evaluation.

Baderin (2003) challenges the argument that the observance of international human rights law is impossible within an Islamic legal framework. Muslim states do not plead Sharia as justification for failure to implement human rights obligations. They do not usually argue against the letter of the law but against some interpretation of international human rights law, which according to them, does not take Islamic values into account. The main question that arises is how far international human rights law can be interpreted in light of Islamic law and also how far Islamic law can be interpreted to account for international human rights law. There is necessity for a synthesis between two extremes and the need for an alternative perspective to the relationship between Islamic law and international human rights law. With evidence from international human rights practice and Islamic jurisprudence, Baderin (2003) confronts the argument that observance of international human rights law is not possible within an Islamic legal dispensation. There is theoretical dialogue between Islamic jurisprudence and international human rights practice. It sets forth a dialogical approach on this issue, one that demands a culture of persuasion and tolerance as opposed to a culture of rivalry, parochialism, and violence. It requires the capacity to listen, accommodate, respect, and exchange.

Many Muslim supporters of the incompatibility view are not, in principle, opposed to the concept of human rights per se. Their view indicates a disappointment and protest towards Western hegemony and consequently any ideology that is apparently championed by the Western nations. They point to the double standards by the West and the overall disparity in reactions to human rights abuses under Islamic and non-Islamic regimes as evidence of a lack of sincerity for human rights. In nearly all human rights resolutions adopted at all Islamic conferences the issue of Palestine invariably comes up as an example of the double standards that are adopted in international relations and law. One critic has denounced the UDHR thus:

> Our history of civilization has taught us to be wary of big and noble words as the reality of our history has taught us how big words can be transformed into atrocious crimes. We cannot forget that the initiators of the Declaration of Human Rights and the plain French citizens are the same people who shortly afterwards and before the ink of the Declaration had dried up, organized a campaign and sent their forces under the leadership of their favorite general, Napoleon, to Egypt. We must not forget also that the United Nations organization issued the Universal Declaration of Human Rights in the same year that it recognized the Zionist state that usurped Palestine and robbed its people of every right stipulated in the Declaration, along with the right to life (Sayf al-Dawla 1988).

As opposed to these four perspectives on human rights and Islamic law, others (Halliday 1995; Baderin 2003) have delineated the following five categories of Islamic responses to the international human rights discourse.

1. Islam is compatible with international human rights.
2. True human rights can only be fully realized under Islamic law.
3. The international human rights objective is an imperialist agenda that should be rejected.
4. Islam is incompatible with human rights.
5. International human rights has a hidden anti-religious agenda.

The importance of adopting a dialogical approach in achieving a common understanding of human rights was reflected in the conclusions adopted by the following conferences.

The Seminar on Human Rights in Islam, held in Kuwait in 1980, which was jointly organized by the International Commission of Jurists, the University of Kuwait, and the Union of Arab Lawyers. The conclusion reached was that: It is unfair to judge Islamic law (Sharia) by the political systems which prevailed in various periods of Islamic history. It ought to be judged by the general principles that are derived from its sources .... Regrettably enough, contemporary Islamic practices cannot be said to conform in many aspects with the true principles of Islam. Furthermore, it is wrong to abuse Islam by seeking to justify certain political systems in the face of obvious contradictions between those systems and Islamic law (International Commission of Jurists 1980).

The Council of Europe at the conclusion of its inter-regional meeting that was organized prior to the World Conference on Human Rights at Strasbourg in 1993, came to the conclusion that we must go back to listening. More thought and effort must be given to enriching the human rights discourse by explicit reference to other nonwestern religions and cultural traditions. By tracing the linkages between constitutional values on the one hand and the concepts, ideas, and institutions that are central to Islam, or the Hindu/Buddhist tradition or other traditions, the base of support for fundamental rights can be expanded and the claim to universality vindicated. The Western world has no monopoly or patent on basic human rights. We must embrace cultural diversity but not at the expense of universal minimum standards (Robinson 1993; Council of Europe 1993).

Furthermore, the fourth principle of the Rome Declaration on Human Rights in Islam, which was issued after the World Symposium on Human Rights by the Muslim World League in February 2000, put forward the need to encourage dialogue between civilizations and cultures in order to contribute to a better understanding of human rights (Rome Declaration 2000).

The International Bill of Human Rights

The Universal Declaration of Human Rights (UDHR) was the first U.N. document that contained a list of internationally recognized human rights. In 1948 it was adopted via a simple resolution of the General Assembly of the United Nations. Later in 1966, two covenants were adopted and they came into force in 1976. These were the International Covenant on Civil and Political Rights (ICCPR) and the International Covenant on Economic, Social, and Cultural Rights (ICESCR). The UDHR along with these two covenants constitutes the International Bill of Rights. Along with these there are two more protocols: the First optional Protocol to the International Covenant on Civil and Political Rights, and the Second optional Protocol to the International Covenant on Civil and Political Rights aiming at the abolition of the Death Penalty. The rights that are guaranteed by the covenants cover most of the basic values that are cherished by every civilized human society. Regional bodies such as the League of Arab States have also adopted various regional human rights treatises to recognize the noble ideals of international human rights. Some of those pertinent to the Muslim World are the Arab Charter on Human Rights (1994), and the Cairo Declaration on Human Rights in Islam adopted by the Organization of Islamic Conference in 1990.

Some human rights scholars have classified human rights according to these being first generation, second generation, or third generation rights (Harris 1998; Sohn 1982).

Under the first generation of rights are the civil and political rights; see Fig. 4.2. These are the traditional rights with respect to liberty and justice that all individuals are entitled to expect from the state. The ICCPR enumerates a list of internationally recognized civil and political rights. Except for the right to self-determination, the civil and political rights are mainly individual rights that every individual is entitled to demand from the state. Formerly, these rights were sought via civil disobedience and revolution. Presently, international human rights law gives the individual legal channels to demand and guarantee these rights. Under the second generation of rights would fall the social, economic, and cultural rights. States are exhorted to take positive action to promote these rights. These are referred to as the enjoyment

Generation	Type	Nature	Remedies
First generation	Civil and political	Individual rights	Civil disobedience; revolution
Second generation	Social, economic and cultural	Enjoyment and sustenance rights	Utopian; directive; non enforceable
Third generation	Collective rights	Solidarity rights	Ancillary rights

Fig. 4.2 Levels of human rights

or sustenance rights, and are forcefully advocated by the developing and socialist nations. The ICESCR lists the internationally recognized social, economic, and cultural rights. In spite of the inevitability of these rights, for the sustenance of human dignity, these social, economic, and cultural rights are regarded as utopian aspirations and considered to be nonlegal and nonjusticiable (Cranston 1973). According to Shue (1996) justice and international law require rich nations to share their abundant resources with the millions of human beings who are chronically malnourished all over the world. The third generation of human rights is ancillary to the above human rights. These are collective rights. These are defined as the solidarity rights, which are based on the solidarity between individuals.

Scholars at a London conference found that aspects of Islamic law are protective of human rights and they recommended that its committee on Islamic law and international law continue its efforts on the contribution of Islamic law to the development of international law by undertaking further studies (Vasak 1979).

Most countries in the Muslim world derive legitimacy from portraying an adherence to Islamic law and traditions. Any effort at enforcing international or universal norms within Muslim societies without consideration to established Islamic law and traditions leads to tension and reactions against the secular nature of the international regime, irrespective of how humane or lofty these international norms may be. Though the political and legal philosophy of Islam could differ in some respects from that of the secular international order, this does not necessarily translate into a complete discord with the international human rights regime. Removing the traditional barriers of distrust and apathy show that diversity is not synonymous with incompatibility. The Islamic heritage, according to Mayer (1999) provides many philosophical concepts, moral principles, and humanistic values that are well adapted to be used in constructing human rights principles. These values and principles abound even in the pre-modern Islamic intellectual heritage. These Islamic humanistic concepts and values of the Sharia should be revived fully for the realization of international human rights within the application of Islamic law in Muslim states.

Purpose of Sharia

Presently, Islamic law is applied in many parts of the Muslim world in its classical forms by both Sunni and Shia Muslims. Analysis reveals that the earliest Islamic jurists employed the methods of Islamic law from within the scope of the Sharia, in a constructive and evolutionary manner so as to preclude any unwarranted circumspection of humans living during their times. This constructive and evolutionary application is very much needed today. With reference to the object and purpose of the Sharia (Maqasid al-Sharia), this has been identified as being the promotion of human welfare and the prevention of harm (Maslahah). This can be considered as an important and holistic approach for realizing the appropriate and benevolent scope of Islamic law (Masud 1995; al-Shatibi 2005). According to Hallaq (1997), al-Shatibi believed that the original intention of God in revealing the law was to protect the religious and the mundane interests of human beings. The following verse of the Quran is offered to support this view. "To each among you have we prescribed a law and an open way, that is, an approach for its application" (Q5:48; Sura Al-Maidah; The Table Spread).

This Maqasid approach for interpreting and applying the Sharia is recognized as guaranteeing the full equity of Islamic law. Furthermore, the following Quranic verse aptly summarizes the benevolent nature of Islamic law. "For He commands them what is just and forbids them what is evil; he allows them as lawful what is good and prohibits them from what is bad. He releases them from their heavy burdens and from the yokes that are upon them" (Q7:157; Al Araf; The Heights).

The Concept of Maslahah

Of the various principles and doctrines that have been established by the founding jurists towards an intelligible application of Islamic law, Maslahah is regarded as the most viable means for bringing the ideals of Islam nearer to realization. Kamali (1988) regards the doctrine of maslahah as broad enough to encompass in its fold, various objectives, both idealist and pragmatic, in order to nurture the standards of good government, and aid in developing the much needed public confidence in the authority of statutory legislation in Muslim societies. This doctrine of maslahah furnishes a balance between the highly idealistic levels of expectation from the government by the public and the efforts of the public to identify more meaningfully with Islam.

The doctrine of maslahah was originally introduced by Imam Malik from the Maliki School of Islamic jurisprudence. Later, it was further developed by jurists such as al-Ghazali, of the Shafeii School (Shafeii 1983) and al-Tufi of the Hanbali School. During the fourteenth century, Abu Ishaq al-Shatibi, of the Maliki School further developed this concept as a basis of rationality and extendibility of Islamic law (Masud 1995). The doctrine of maslahah can be considered to be an expedient doctrine of Islamic law, and is regarded by Islamic legalists as containing the seeds of the future of the Sharia and its viability as a living force in society.

The term maslahah literally means welfare or benefit, and is generally applied under Maliki jurisprudence, in a narrower sense, to express the principle of public welfare or public benefit, and is often qualified as "maslahah mursalah" (released benefit), if the benefit is not tied down to a specific textual authority but is based on considerations of collective well-being. In this sense, maslahah has often been understood to mean "maslahah al-ummah," or the benefit or welfare of the Muslim community as a whole. However, the utility of maslahah towards achieving the communal welfare does not preclude its broader application to protect the rights and welfare of individuals. Generally, the concept of maslahah further accommodates the doctrine of Maslahah shakhsiyyah or individual benefit/welfare in order to protect human rights. Because human rights specifically seek to protect the rights of individuals, its ultimate goal is also to guarantee the benefit and welfare of human beings as a whole. Furthermore, protecting the welfare of individuals eventually ensures communal/public welfare and vice versa. This makes the doctrine of Maslahah very relevant while discussing human rights under Islamic law.

While looking at the overall objective of maslahah with respect to the Sharia (maqasid al-Sharia), al-Shatibi built upon the theory of al-Ghazali to set up a three-step hierarchical classification for determining the scope of maslahah. See Fig 4.3. At the first or highest level are the five universals (Hallaq 1997): protection of life, religion, intellect, family, and property. Due to their importance these need to be not only promoted but also protected. Contemporary Muslim scholars (Kamali 1993) consider these to be fundamental rights (al-huquq al-fitriyyah). At the second level are those rights that are regarded as necessary benefits (hajiyyat). These may be regarded as supplementary to the first category and constitute those benefits, whose neglect may cause hardship to life. However, the neglect of these may not necessarily lead to a collapse of society. These rights ensure accommodation of necessary changes in life within the ambit of the law and thus make life more tolerable. At the third level are those rights that are regarded as improvement benefits (tahsiniyyat) and consist of those amenities that improve and embellish life generally and thus enhance the overall character of the Sharia (Hallaq 1997; Nyazee 2000; Kamali 1993; Masud 1989).

In light of the above, the doctrine of maslahah may be implemented for the realization of international human rights from within the dispensation of Islamic law. International human rights have a universal humanitarian objective to protect individuals against misuse of state authority and enhancement of human dignity. The doctrine of maslahah, from within the Sharia can be utilized to carve out rights by deriving legal benefits and avert hardship on human beings by relying on the following Quranic verse: "He has not imposed any hardships upon you in religion" (Q22:78; Sura Al-Hajj; the Pilgrimage).

Employing maslahah from within the maqasid al-Sharia can accommodate the principle of takhayyur, eclectic choice (Coulson 1969), so as to facilitate movement within the main schools of Islamic jurisprudence, along with a consideration of the views of individual Islamic jurists to support alternative arguments.

Level	Category	Scope	Action/function
First	Five universals	Fundamental rights	Promoted and protected by state
Second	Hajiyyat	Supplementary rights	Neglect leads to hardship; accommodates social change
Third	Tahsiniyyat	Improvement benefits	Enhances character of the Sharia

Fig. 4.3 Hierarchical scope of Maslahah

Presently, interpretations of the Sharia in the Muslim world are classified into two main divisions, the traditionalist and the evolutionist. Traditionalists see value in tenaciously holding on to the classical interpretations of the Sharia from that which was laid down in the legal treatises of the established schools of Islamic jurisprudence of the tenth century. They are also referred to as hardliners or conservatives due to their strict adherence to the classical legal treatises. On the other hand, the evolutionists are those who, besides identifying with the classical jurisprudence and methods of Islamic law, also attempt to make it relevant to contemporary times. This group believes in the continual evolution of Islamic law and avers that in order to cope meaningfully with modern developments, and be applicable for all time, the Sharia should take modern developments into consideration. This group may be referred to as the Islamic moderates or liberals. In an attempt to harmonize international human rights law and Islamic law, the main issue is whether one adopts a hardline or a moderate approach in interpreting the Sharia and the application of classical Islamic jurisprudence.

The Justificatory Principle

The most robust arguments for the universality of human rights rest on moral arguments and the requirement of substantive justice in human relationships. It takes into consideration values and beliefs that do not change over time and space. Baderin (2003) examines justificatory arguments with respect to the values that are attached to certain human rights from the Islamic law and international human rights perspectives. This approach would help in getting a better understanding into the areas of differences and furnish a basis for the practical harmonization of the conceptual differences between Islamic law and international human rights principles.

Western nations generally view human rights to be the product of western liberalism, which advocates for the values of freedom, liberty, individualism, and tolerance. However, many Muslim nations consider Western liberalism to be too permissive and capable of corrupting the moral values of their societies as prescribed by the Sharia. Considering liberalism and human rights as vehicles for total liberty and freedom of the individual to do whatever one desires is wrong because it will contradict the basic foundations of legal and political authority. The need for control by the political authority through law is recognized, but the limitations that are imposed upon individual freedoms and liberties, should be justified according to the law and not used arbitrarily. The justificatory principle sets up restrictions upon individual rights based on clearly determinable and justifiable criteria so as not to violate individual freedom, liberty, and fundamental human rights.

With respect to Islamic law, the political authority has a duty to the people and to God, to abstain from violating the freedom and liberties of the ruled without justification. This justificatory principle has support in the Quran because a justifying clause comes along with nearly all prohibitions concerning human relations (muamalat). The parameters of justification, from an Islamic legal perspective, can be found within the Quran. Though the text of the Quran cannot be amended, its provisions can be interpreted with respect to societal changes and the relevant justificatory principle from the holistic values of the Sharia. In light of this an Islamic legal maxim states that: "tatagayyar al-ahkam fi tagayur al-Zaman," legal rulings may change with the change in time (al-Ghanaimi 1968). This applies to matters pertaining to human interactions (muamalat) and examples of these can be found throughout the ages in the practices of Muslim jurists. Islamic evolutionists adopt this approach while interpreting Islamic legal texts, because it facilitates accommodation with the dynamic changes of human life. They reason that when the justification for certain legal provisions change, then the legal rules may also change. A good example of this may be found in the Nigerain case of Tela Rijiyan Dorawa v. Hassan Daudu (1975 Nigerian Law Report 87).

This was a case in Nigeria which has a multireligious population, with Muslims in the majority. The Nigerian judicial system functions as a pluralized legal system with English law, Islamic law, and customary law. This case involved a land dispute between a Christian plaintiff and a Muslim defendant. Each party called a witness to give evidence on their behalf. Upon review of the evidence the trial court rejected the testimony of the Christian because the testimony of a non-Muslim was not acceptable under Islamic law. The Christian plaintiff appealed to the High Court. The learned High Court judge, a Muslim, on consultation from the Grand Qadi, allowed the appeal and overturned the ruling of the lower court that prohibited the testimony of a Christian. In its decision the High Court relied on the Islamic legal principle of takhayyur (eclectic choice) which permits reliance on the opinions of other Islamic Schools of jurisprudence. It also examined Islamic legal literature to show that the traditional reason for the disqualification of testimony of non-Muslims by the classical Islamic jurists was the fear of their being unjust because of their lack of Islamic belief and their evidence was acceptable when there was an absence of any fear or due to necessity. The court looked into the condition of present-day Nigeria as a country with large Muslim, animist, and Christian communities that live and have business transactions with each other. This fact was sufficient to satisfy the necessity of making the evidence of a non-Muslim admissible under Islamic law (Muhammad 1992).

Human Rights in the Globalized Context

Johnston (2007) delineates three distinct recent trends among Muslim scholars regarding the issue of human rights. Muhammad al-Ghazali and Muhammad Amara constitute the traditionalists. Muhammad Talbi, Muhammad al-Matawakkal, and Rashid al-Ghannushi are categorized as the progressive conservatives. Ebrahim Moosa and Khalid Abu El Fadl are regarded as the progressives working with a postmodern epistemology. According to Johnston (2007), this move highlights a trend towards ethical objectivism and an epistemological inclination of ethical values over certain formulations of the text that could facilitate a greater number of conservatives and progressives towards convergence on the burning current issues of human rights.

A careful analysis of various accounts by Islamic scholars reveals that human rights are an endowment for all mankind simply by virtue of their creation; The concept of rights that are advocated by the UDHR are virtually the same as those taught by Islam. This implies that the UDHR meets the approval of Muslims when their legal framework is properly interpreted (Kurzman 1998). What has changed since the crystallization of fiqh is the international context. The Quranic concept of humanity's trusteeship requires a legal framework to implement the spirit of the sharia in the context of today's globalized society.

Muslim scholars living in the West contend that the entire relationship between Islamic theology and the law must be thoroughly rethought and reworked. Sachedina (2001) contends that those seeking to apply the corpus of Islamic law entirely intact since medieval times in the present context has been problematic since this epistemology has resulted in many of the apologetic works. As a consequence, these have further mystified the real purpose of Islamic institutions and their revival in modern times. The demand for a sharia-compliant state has bypassed the need to re-examine religious epistemology which necessitates extensive rethinking before it can provide guidance for Muslims in the modern nation state. The ethics of the Quran need to be re-examined from the normative tradition whereby Islamic law employs istihsan (judgments of equity) and maslahah (public interest) for the common good whereby ethical theology promotes human reason to discern right from wrong.

Amara, one of the enlightened Islamists is in some respects atypical of modern Islamists who call for a certain extent of pluralism as necessary for the Islamic community, so far as it conforms to the general welfare of the umma, which is the purpose of the sharia. According to this Egyptian intellectual, Islam is the religion of the original human nature (din al fitra). From a western perspective, human rights are only optional sociopolitical and cultural privileges. However, under Islam the entitlement of human beings is a moral necessity (Kramer 1999).

Rashid Ghannushi believes that a return to Islam does not imply isolation from the world around us or from people who believe differently. Actually, Islam calls for people to live together, cooperate, and foster dialogue in order to enhance the values of freedom, democracy, and justice. Not only are these Muslim values but they are also human values (Dwyer 1991).

According to Ramadan (2004), the classical fiqh vision whereby the world was divided into dar al Islam and dar al haram, was an attempt to circumscribe the operation of the law in time and space, but this categorization is now obsolete. With change it is now necessary to go back to the Quran and the Sunna, considering the new environment, and broaden our analysis so as to develop a new vision that is in consonance with our new situation in order to formulate suitable legal opinions. He advises Muslims to shake off their double inferiority complex (from western culture and patronage from certain Muslim countries) and participate actively in the ethical debates like fully engaged citizens of their respective countries. This will result in Muslims being able to claim their legal rights, and also contribute tremendously towards the ethical, religious, and social values for the benefit of their host societies.

Ramadan along with al-Ghannushi recommends the following theological/legal building blocks: maslahah, ijtihad, fatwa. Conceptualizing what is in the public interest (maslaha), formulating new legal rules that cover new situations (ijtihad), that are based on the texts and methodologies of Islamic legal tradition, and promulgation of rulings in answer to specific requests (fatwa). These are the essential tools via which Muslim communities in any society can adapt and evolve in the context of sociopolitical realities.

With ongoing changes in social organization and categorization of groups the organizational base has gradually shifted from land/nation state to one based on culture/interest via blogs and social networking. There is an increasing emergence of newer forms of social cleavages and groups. There are a growing number of emerging transnational groups/organizations. This phenomenon is also being increasingly seen in Muslim communities ranging from Al-Qaeda to the recent protest movements in Arab countries. The challenge for organizational control and normative grounding of these aggregates would require new methods of consensus building and governance and also a new institutional apparatus for its administration. It is here that the M-I-F (maslahah, ijtihad, fatwa) process shows promise for Muslim communities.

Notes

1. The term Muslim States needs to be defined. Muslim world is currently divided into separate sovereign nation states. Some of these have been specifically declared to be Islamic Republics; others indicate in their constitutions that Islam is the state religion, and many identify themselves only as Muslim states on the basis of their predominant Muslim population and allegiance to Islam. Another criterion adopted by Baderin (2003) for defining modern Muslim states is membership in the Organization of Islamic Conference (OIC). All 57 member states of the OIC are defined as Muslim states and are supported by the first charter objective of the OIC, which is the promotion of Islamic spiritual, ethical, social, and economic values among the member states. Although OIC member states exist as independent sovereign states, they are theoretically connected by their

Islamic heritage, traditions, and solidarity. With respect to the application of Islamic law as state law, Esposito (1999) notes that a majority of Muslim states today fall between two extremes: purist Saudi Arabia or secular Turkey.

2. The maxim: *Rahmah al-Ummah fi Ikhtilaf al-A'immah* (The blessing of the Muslim Community lies in the jurists' differences of opinion). This reveals that differences of opinion by the jurists with regard to the interpretation of legal sources on some matters reveals a broad and equally legal scope from which judges can choose the most compassionate and beneficial opinion from cases that they encounter before them. It was based on this maxim that the Islamic legal principle of takhayyur (eclectic choice) evolved and called for unification within the different schools of Islamic jurisprudence (Coulson 1969). Abu Abdullah al-Dimashqi, a fifteenth century jurist, wrote a jurisprudential book titled *Rahmah al-ummah fi Ikhtilaf al-A'immah* wherein he listed the legal consensus and discussion of the classical jurists.

3. Muslims consist of two main groups, Shiah and Sunni. The Shiah constitute about 10% while the Sunni are the majority of the world Muslim population. The Shiah group arose due to a schism among Muslims regarding succession, during the caliphate of Ali. With respect to Sunni Islam, there are six authentic books containing the collections of the Prophet's traditions. These books have been written by al-Bukhari (d.870 AD), al-Tirmidhi (d. 892 AD), al-Nasai (d. 915 AD), and Ibn Majah (d. 886 AD). The Shiah too have their own collections of the Prophet's traditions, such as al-Kafi by Abu Jafar al-Kulayni al Razi (d. 939 AD) and al-Istibsar by Abu Jafar al-Tusi (d. 971 AD).

4. In order to get a proper understanding of the nature of Islamic law one should be able to make a distinction between Sharia and Fiqh. Although either of the terms Fiqh and Sharia are used interchangeably when referring to Islamic law, they are not technically synonymous. Sharia literally means path to be followed or right path (Doi 1984), whereas Fiqh means understanding (Quran 45:18). The prophet used Fiqh in one of his sayings to imply understanding," to whomsoever God wishes good. He gives the understanding (Fiqh) of the faith." Fiqh is also used in the Quran to mean understanding (Q9:87). Sharia mainly refers to the sources, whereas Fiqh refers to the methods of Islamic law. From the legal perspective, Sharia comprises the corpus of the revealed law as it is contained in the Quran along with the authentic traditions of the Prophet (the Sunnah). It varies in this sense from Fiqh because Sharia refers to the primary sources of the law, which is textually immutable. On the other hand Fiqh refers to the methods of the law, which is the understanding one derives from, and the application of the Sharia, which is subject to change due to circumstances and time (Ramadan 1970; Philips 1988).

Respect for justice, along with protection of dignity and human life are the main principles that are inherent in the Sharia and these are not subject to exclusion due to differences of opinion. According to the Quran, the main purpose of the Sharia is: God commands justice, the doing of good, and liberality to kith and kin, and he forbids all shameful deeds, and injustice and rebellion: He instructs you that you may receive admonition. (Q16:90).

References

Al-Ghunaimi, M. T. (1968). *The Muslim conception of international law and the Western approach.* The Hague: Nijhoff.

An-Na'im, A. A. (1990). *Towards an Islamic reformation, civil liberties, human rights, and international law.* New York: Syracuse University Press.

Baderin, M. A. (2003). *International human rights and Islamic law.* New York: Oxford University Press.

Coulson, N. J. (1969). *Conflicts and tension in Islamic jurisprudence.* Chicago: University of Chicago Press.

Cranston, M. (1973). *What are human rights?* London: The Bodley Head.

David, R. (1975). Introduction. In R. David (Ed.), *International Encyclopedia of comparative law, II.* Tubingen: J.C.B. Mohr.

Doi, A. R. (1984). Shariah: The Islamic Law. London. Ta Ha Publishers.

Dwyer, K. (1991). *Arab voices: The human rights debate in the Middle East.* London/New York: Routledge.

Esposito, J. L. (1999). Contemporary Islam: Reformation or Revolution, in Esposito, J.L., (ed.) The Oxford History of Islam. Oxford: Oxford University Press.

Hallaq, W. B. (1997). *A history of Islamic legal theories.* Cambridge: Cambridge University Press.

Halliday, F. (1995). Relativism and universalism in human rights: The case of the Islamic Middle East. In D. Beetham (Ed.), *Politics and human rights.* Oxford: Blackwell.

Harris, D. J. (1998). *Cases and materials on international law.* London: Sweet and Maxwell.

Johnston, D. (2007). Maqasid Al-Sharia: Epistemology and hermeneutics of Muslim theologies of human rights. *Die Welt des Islams, 47*(2), 149–187.

Kamali, M. H. (1988). Have we neglected the Sharia – Law doctrine of Maslahah? *Islamic Studies, 27*(4), 287–288.

Kamali, M. H. (1993). Fundamental rights of the individual: An analysis of Haqq (rights) in Islamic law. *American Journal of Islamic Social Sciences, 10*(3), 340.

Kramer, G. (1999). *Gottes Staat als Republik: Reflexionen zeitgenossischer Muslime Zu Islam, Menschenrechten und Deomcratie.* Baden-Baden: Nomos Verlagsgessellschaft.

Kurzman, C. (1998). Muslim participation in a non-Muslim state. In C. Kurzman (Ed.), *Liberal Islam: A sourcebook.* London/New York: Oxford University Press.

Masud, M. K. (1989). *Islamic legal philosophy: A study of Abu Ishaq al-Shatibi's life and thought.* Delhi: International Islamic Publishers.

Masud, M. K. (1995). *Shatibi's philosophy of Islamic law.* Islamabad: Islamic Research Institute.

Mayer, A. E. (1999). *Islam and human rights: Tradition and politics.* Boulder: Westview Press.

Monshipouri, M. (1998). *Islamism, secularism, and human rights in the Middle East.* Boulder: L. Rienner.

Muhammad, Hon. Justice U. (1992). Sharia and the Western common law: A comparative Analysis. In M. O. Abdul Rahman (Ed.), Thoughts in Islamic law and ethics. Ibadan: University of Ibadan Muslim Graduates Association.

Nyazee, I. A. K. (2000). *Outlines of Islamic jurisprudence.* Islamabad: Advanced Legal Study Institute.

Philips, A. A. B. (1988). *The evolution of Fiqh.* Riyadh: International Islamic Publishing House.

Quraishi, A. (2000). A book review of Islamism, secularism, and human rights in the Middle East by Mahmood Monshipouri. *Human Rights Quarterly, 22,* 265.

Ramadan, S. (1970). *Islamic law: Its scope and equity.* London: McMillan.

Ramadan, T. (2004). *Western Muslims and the future of Islam.* London/New York: Oxford University Press.

Robinson, M. (1993). Human rights at the dawn of the 21st century. *Human Rights Quarterly, 15,* 629, at p. 632.

Rosen, L. (2000). *The justice of Islam.* Oxford/New York: Oxford University Press.

Sachedina, A. (1993). Review of Abdellahi Ahmed An-Na'im, towards and Islamic reformation: Civil liberties, human rights and international law. *International Journal of Middle East Studies*, *25*, 155.

Sachedina, A. (2001). *The Islamic roots of democratic pluralism*. Oxford/New York: Oxford University Press.

Sayf al-DawlaR, I. (1988). Islam and human rights: Controversy and agreement (1985) 9 Minbar al-Hiwar pp 33–39 cited in al-Sayyid R. (1995). Contemporary Muslim thought and human rights. *Islamochristiana, 21*, p.27.

Shafeii, M. (1983). al-Risala, Cairo: Mustafa al-Babi al-Halabi.

Shue, H. (1996). *Basic rights: Subsistence, affluence and US foreign policy*. Princeton: Princeton University Press.

Sohn, L. B. (1982). The new international law: Protection of the rights of individuals rather than states. *American University Law Journal, 32*, 1–64.

Tela Rijiyan Dorawa v. Hassan Daudu (1975) Nigerian Law Report, 87.

Troll, C. W. (1992). Book review of Islam and human rights: Traditions and politics by Ann Elizabeth Mayer. *Islam and Christian-Muslim Relations, 3*(1), 131.

Vasak, K. (1979). *For the third generation of human rights; The right of solidarity*. Paper delivered at the 10th study session of the International Institute of Human Rights, Strasbourg, 2–27 July 1979.

Documents/Reports

Council of Europe Document CE/CMDH (93) 16, of 30 Jan 1993, at p. 3.

Rome Declaration on Human Rights in Islam (2000). 4th Principle.

International Commission of Jurists, Human Rights in Islam. Report of a seminar held in Kuwait in December 1980 (1982) p. 7.

Arabic Sources

Abuzahrah, Muhammad (1974) Al-Jarimah wa Al-Uqubah Fi Al-Fiqh al-Islami (crime and punishment in Islamic Jurisprudence). Cairo: Dar al-Fikr al-Arabi.

Al Dimashqi, Abu Abdullah(1995) Rahmah al-ummah fi Ikhtilaf al-A'immah. Beirut: Dal Kutub al Ilmiyyah.

Al-Shatibi, Abu Ishaq (2005) Muwafaqat fi usool al-Sharia. Dar ul Kutub al-Ilmiyya.

Al-Ghazali, M (1356 AH) al Mustasfa fi Ilm al usul. Cairo: maktabah al- Tijariyyah.

Al-Ghunaimi, MT (1961) Durus fi usul al-Qaanun al-wadai cited in Al-Ghunaimi, M.T. (1968) The Muslim Conception of International Law and the Western Approach. The Hague: Nijhoff.

Chapter 5
Police and the Administration of Justice in Medieval India

Introduction

This chapter outlines one of the case studies of policing by Muslims. It examines the system of policing and administration of justice applied in India first, during the period of the Delhi Sultanates (1206–1526 CE) and later during the Mughal era (1526–1860 CE).

Scholars of policing have classified policing structures based on the concepts of decentralization and centralization with respect to worldwide policing structures. Bayley (1985) enunciates two dimensions of analysis that are necessary to describe adequately the structure of police systems around the world. These are based on the type of command structure (centralized/decentralized); and the number of forces to be supervised (single/multiple). This typology has utility because it helps researchers understand relationships among countries. It can also have utility by examining the structure of a country over time. According to Bayley's analytical scheme, policing under Islamic systems tends to be singular and highly centralized. Under this analytical system Saudi Arabia's police system is a centralized single type of system, but it has some pockets of tribal authority. Normally local and informal methods are used before resorting to the formal police apparatus in Saudi Arabia. The Saudis use the *mutawwiun* to ensure strict compliance to the tenets of Islam. Formal policing in Saudi Arabia is situated in the Ministry of the Interior. The director of public safety is subordinate to the minister. This director is appointed by the king and is responsible for all the police forces in Saudi Arabia (Alobeid 1989; Kurian 1989).

Sultanate Period

With respect to India, there is a similar centralized single model. The first Muslim incursions occurred via Sindh in the beginning of the eighth century CE Most of these early incursions were not permanent and did not have much impact on the

F.B. Hakeem et al., *Policing Muslim Communities: Comparative International Context*,
DOI 10.1007/978-1-4614-3552-5_5, © Springer Science+Business Media New York 2012

Indian political landscape. Later incursions by Turks, Persians, and Afghans, during the eleventh century had a greater impact. During the following three centuries most of the northern part of India came under their sway. According to Muslim chroniclers, the police duties were performed by the kotwal, whose office was identical to that of the *Sahabi Shurtah* of the caliphate. During the sultanate period, the kotwal was assisted by the local inhabitants and an elite civil force, which patrolled the streets and guarded the city.

The kotwal functioned as a committing magistrate and administered the rural areas too. Sometimes the kotwal also had the task of a military commander of a fort. The Muhtasib was an official who performed most of the normal policing functions. He was expected to control illegal activities and was required to maintain a high code of conduct of public behavior. During this era, the Muhtasib had a complex set of duties. He functioned as an inspector general of police, a chief engineer of public works, along with being an inspector of public morals. In the cities, the Muhtasib delegated his duties to the kotwal. The duties of the kotwal required him to be ever vigilant. Regular police forces along with spies were employed. Prominent citizens were appointed as wardens for every quarter of the city. The force that was under his command was a purely civil one. The Muhtasib was essentially an executive officer, while the Qazi was a purely judicial officer who had the task of interpreting and administering the sacred law. One of the unique features of the sultanate period was that a single person simultaneously held the offices of the kotwal and the Muhtasib. The Amir-i-dad controlled the offices of Muhtasib and kotwal and was the most important official during this period.

Mughal Period

An examination of the police structure in Mughal India, which was an Islamic system, also reveals a very centralized structure. According to Bayley's classification this structure can be characterized as a centralized single structure.

Most of our information about the system of policing in Mughal India comes from European travelers who visited India during the sixteenth and seventeenth centuries (Bernier 1891; Manucci 1966; Tavernier 1889; Mandelslo 1995). They related that the Mughals did not have any law and that the administration of justice was accomplished in a very elementary and summary manner. These accounts are not accurate and are based on the ignorance of these travelers about the laws and documents of this period, which were mostly in Persian. Many official documents (imperial gazettes and newsletters) of the Mughal emperors were submerged in the official chronicles of the period. Most of these were in Persian and were usually scattered across the country. Due to such a disarray of these sources no attempt was made to evaluate them and discern a picture of judicial organization and practice. Most studies of this period were based on English and Urdu translations of these Persian chronicles supplemented with the accounts of the European travelers.

The Mughal dynasty began in 1526 AD when Babur conquered some parts of northern India. This dynasty was to have a lasting impact on the administrative apparatus of India. The system of policing that the Mughals established lasted for more than 300 years and was gradually replaced after the Mutiny of 1857. Though the Mughal Empire began to wane after the death of Aurangzeb in 1707, the system of Sharia continued to be applied with the support of the police system until 1860. Since the British had initially come to India as traders under the auspices of the East India Company, they left the administration up to the Mughals and other Indian rulers. The policing and administrative system set up by the Mughal emperors continued to be applied until the Indian Police Act was passed in 1861. Although the police later followed the model of the Irish Constabulary system it still retained many of its Mughal elements in the Mofussils (nonmetropolitan areas). In spite of having defeated the Mughals, the British still had to maintain some elements of the Mughal Islamic system because it had much more cultural affinity with Indian society than the British system.

In order to get a better estimation of the system of policing and administration of justice there are various sources that give an account of this period. These sources may be summarized as follows.

(a) Official Mughal records
(b) Printed Persian works
(c) Urdu translations of Persian works
(d) English translations of Persian works
(e) Hindi works
(f) Accounts by Westerners.

Official Mughal Records

The imperial Mughals set up a fairly advanced and mechanized system of government in India. Due to the increase in administrative functions and civic responsibilities by the state, the rule of law was established. As a consequence, the Mughal emperors increasingly relied on the written word in managing their dominions. There was a gradual accumulation of records, which were not known during the reign of the sultans of Delhi. Realizing the significance of preserving these records in a systematic manner, Emperor Akbar created the Public Records Office in 1574. He began the practice of recording the minutes of the proceedings of his court chronologically for future reference. Initially, 14 clerks were appointed for this purpose. Two of them were on duty on each day of the week. Similar to the modern day stenographers, they scribbled notes of all that happened at the imperial court during the day that was allotted to them. Upon approval of the final draft of the proceedings by the sovereign, its multiple copies were prepared by the calligraphists for the purpose of distribution among the courtiers, feudatories, and the provincial governors. Private citizens were entitled to get copies of these proceedings upon request. The minutes of the proceedings were called the Akhbarat (plural for Akhbar,

the newspaper), viz the news of the imperial court or the newsletters. These documents constitute the very raw materials of Mughal history. Emperor Akbar introduced this practice which was highly modern in its concept and import. It can be
compared with the modern democratic practice of recording the proceedings of the
national parliament and state assemblies and the gazette notification of executive
actions. The akhbarat were akin to mirrors through which all those interested in
court politics, or public affairs, could have a glimpse of all that occurred at the
Mughal court (Mehta 1986).

An examination of these original documents in Persian gives a systematic and
comprehensive account of criminal law and procedure under the Mughal emperors
from 1556 to 1707 (Araiz-o-Farman (newsletters), and Akhbarat-i-Darbar-Mualla
(Imperial Gazettes)). These sources are an invaluable insight into the administrative
practices of the Mughals during this period and provide a valuable contribution to
our knowledge. It further traces the changes of Muslim law in its Indian environment (Sangar 1967).

The Mughal Administrative Structure

The Mughal system took its hue from the race and creed of its sovereigns. They
were a Muslim dynasty that settled in India eight centuries after Islam was adopted
in some countries outside India. The Turkish conquerors that preceded the Mughals
introduced a model of administration that Muslim countries outside India had used.
This model had proved to be a very successful one over the centuries. These were
the administrative system of the Abbasid caliphs of Iraq (750–1258 AD) and the
Fatimid caliphs of Egypt (909–1171 AD). The Indian system was a combination of
both the Persian and the Arab systems in the Indian setting. The imported system
was modified to suit local needs. In this process the existing Indian practices and the
mass of Indian customary laws were respected as long as these did not run counter
to the root principles of Islamic government. Generally, Indian usages were allowed
to prevail in village administration and the lower rungs of officialdom. Emperor
Babar established a policy of religious toleration and advised his son Humayun to
ignore the disputes between the Shia and the Sunnis because therein lay the weakness of Islam. He is recorded to have said that the progress of Islam is better achieved
with the sword of kindness.

The early stages of Arab rule witnessed a distinction between two main political functions in Egypt: the governorship and the treasury. The *amir* (governor)
controlled the military and the police, while the *amil* (treasurer) was the head of
the treasury. Both these officials had to keep a watch on each other. It was a system of checks and balances. As the head of the military and executive the *amir*
was higher in authority but they were equal in rank. In fact, due to the nature of
his functions the *amil* had greater influence over the sovereign at the central level
in Delhi. This relation was duplicated between the *subhedar* (provincial governors) and the *diwan* (revenue chief of province). At the provincial level the *subhedar,*

diwan, and q*azi* followed the procedure of the imperial court. The state was content with police duties and revenue collection. The Mughals left the villagers alone as long as they did not commit violent crimes or defy the royal authority in the region. The *diwan* was the highest functionary below the emperor and there was no council of ministers.

Though the government was military in character it did not change when it became more settled. It retained its military character till the end. All officials in the Mughal government were enrolled in the army list; they were given a *mansab* (command of a number of horsemen) and this determined their pay and status. All administrative officials were ranked as *mansabdars*. Their names were arranged in the gradation list of the army and they were paid by the *bakhshis* (military paymasters) and their promotion resulted in an increase of their nominal command.

The emperor was at the head of the executive. The Mughal system had its roots in the system established by the Delhi sultans who preceded them. Under the Mughals three main agencies accomplished the task of judicial administration. These were the imperial, the judicial (sharia), and the panchayati.

(a) The emperor through his delegates, the subhedar, faujdar, and kotwal dealt with the political cases. These secular officials punished robbers and other rebels who worked in an organized manner.

(b) The *qazi* dealt with the sharia and his jurisdiction was circumscribed only to questions dealing with religion. These included disputes pertaining to marriage and family law, inheritance, *auqaf* (trusts), and criminal cases.

(c) The courts of the Brahmin pandits and caste elders were for the Hindus and other villagers. These were administered according to the common law or traditions of the tribes. They were neither subordinate to the *qazi*, nor were they related to the sharia law. The policing of rural areas was left to the local populace. This task was performed by local *chaukidars* (watchmen) who were employed by the villagers and were servants of the village community. The *chaukidars* were neither paid nor supervised by the state. The local villagers were responsible for the safety of their own property and also of travelers who passed by the roads.

With respect to criminal justice administration the sharia gave wide discretion to the sovereign. However, it is not correct to assume, as many foreign travelers have done in their accounts that the emperors' will was always the law in all matters or that he could act in a capricious fashion. This was the perception conveyed by the foreign travelers who did not fully comprehend the legal system. In one account Careri, erroneously narrated that "The Great Moghul is so absolute that there being no written Laws, his will in all things is law, and last decision of all causes, both civil and criminal. He makes a tyrannical use of his absolute power" (Sen 1949).

The law served as a check on the emperor's capriciousness. He could not go against the sharia without being challenged by orthodox clergy (ulema). If he dared to transgress the sharia he would provoke the wrath of the orthodox Muslims.

Even Emperor Akbar had to face stiff opposition from the orthodox Muslims when he decided to introduce his new religion *Deen-e-Illahi.*

Police Administration

Under this system the *amir* (viceroy) was the most important official, but the *muhtasib* was the official mainly concerned with police administration (Griffiths 1971). During this period the *faujdars* functioned as purely military officers; they exercised control over the military police and acceded to the sovereign's orders within their respective jurisdictions. The *muhtasib* was the chief officer who was responsible for police administration. The *kotwal* assisted the *muhtasib* and was in turn assisted by a number of subordinate officers. The *muhtasib* had manifold duties. Besides being the chief of police he was also the chief engineer of public health, and an inspector of public morals. In the cities he was authorized to delegate his policing duties to the *kotwal.* The umayyuds had adopted the Byzantine agoronomus (market inspector) and assimilated him into Islamic practice, and accorded him more responsibility. The *muhtasib* was responsible for protecting the standards of religious morality and also regulating market affairs.

As a subordinate officer to the *muhtasib,* the *kotwal* had to keep a register of all inhabitants within his jurisdiction. The *muhtasib* also functioned as a committing magistrate. The force under his command was an entirely civil one as opposed to the one under the *faujdar,* which was military. Historical accounts of policing under the Mughal period available through the *Akbarnama, Mirat-e-Ahmadi,* and the *Ain-e-Akbari,* shed further light on the criminal justice system and police administration during this period.

Under the Mughal government, provinces were placed under the *subhedar* who was responsible to the Emperor for overall administration of the province. The main duties of the *subhedar* were to maintain law and order, help towards the smooth and successful collection of revenue, and execute the royal decrees and regulations that were sent to him from the Emperor (Sarkar 1972). The province was divided into *sarkars* (districts), and each *sarkar* was placed under the supervision of the *faujdar,* who was appointed by the Emperor but placed under the supervision of the *subhedar.* The *faujdar* was the chief police officer and the administrative and military head of a *sarkar.* He also was the head of a military contingent that ranged from 500 to 1,500 soldiers. His main functions were to maintain law and order, apprehend criminals, and commit them to a criminal court for trial and punishment. He had executive powers and these enabled him to function as a police magistrate (Saha 1990). The *sarkars* were further divided into *parganas.* The *shikadars* were officials who were in charge of the *pargana* and they were under the control of the faujdars. Each *pargana* was further subdivided into *thanas.* The *thanedars* were subordinate to the *shikadars* and were responsible for the *thanas* and they were assisted by the *barkandazes.* The *thanedars* usually held court in the parganas and were assisted in the court proceedings by the *gumashta* (news-writer), the *chaudharis,* and the *qanungos* (Sangar 1967; see Fig. 5.1).

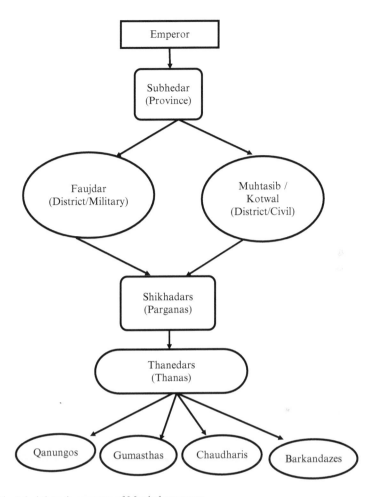

Fig. 5.1 Administrative system of Mughal emperors

Functions and Duties of Kotwals

The *Ain-e-Akbari* gives a lucid account of the varied duties of the *kotwal*. The responsibility for policing in the towns was entrusted to the *kotwals* who were secular functionaries. Besides the regular police duties, they performed the duties of the *muhtasib*. The *kotwals* resembled the present-day inspectors of police. Even today, in many cities of northern India the officers in charge of the city police stations are known as *kotwals* and the police stations that they hold are referred to as *kotwalis*.

The *kotwal* was responsible for the watch and ward duties in the city and was responsible for the control of social evils such as prostitution, distillation of liquor, and the regulation of public gatherings. He had at his service a regular staff of watchmen who patrolled the streets at night. The *kotwal* also had a number of paid informants who kept him informed about all developments in the vicinity. There was much crime that was committed by pickpockets and sneak thieves during the Mughal period and the *kotwal* had to take adequate precautionary measures to curb them at public gatherings (Rao 1967).

Other sources provide us with valuable details about police administration and organization during this period. The appointment *sanad* (decree) of the *kotwal* exhorted him to guarantee that thefts did not occur in the city and that citizens were able to conduct their business peacefully. Since he was an important official, the kotwal had to regularly attend the Emperor's durbar (court). So far as rank was concerned, he was subordinate to the qazi, who dealt with the sacred law and was the judicial representative of the emperor. Manucci (1966) relates that the *kotwal* was subordinate to the qazi, but he commanded a very efficient body of men. "Under the *kotwals'* orders there is a large body of cavalry and many foot soldiers who go on rounds through the city." All sources confirm that there was a higher degree of efficiency of police in towns as opposed to the rural areas that were under the loose control of the *faujdar* who was responsible for its overall supervision.

As chief of the city police, the *kotwal* had to take precautionary measures against crime since he was held accountable for all crimes that occurred in his jurisdiction. He appointed watchmen in every *mohalla* (ward) of the city. These watchmen were on duty during the entire night and had the task of apprehending thieves and other criminals. The watchmen were to guard against pickpockets by patrolling places of entertainment. The *kotwal* also personally patrolled the streets in order to round up thieves.

According to Thevenot (Sen 1949), the *kotwal* was also required to patrol the streets at night. If he encountered any unauthorized person moving around in a suspicious manner he put him in prison and gave him a whipping. During his patrols the *kotwal* was accompanied by three guards, two of them beat little drums and the third sounded a long copper trumpet and shouted a warning cry *khabardaar* (beware). These rounds were performed three times during the night: one at nine o'clock, the second at midnight, and finally at three o'clock in the morning. As a matter of practice the *kotwals* adopted a very proactive approach to combat crime in Mughal India. They were required to take bonds from liquor vendors, dancing girls, and professional women to ensure good conduct. In cases where the bond was not fulfilled the individuals were fined (Sen 1949).

The *Ain* and the *Mirat-i-Ahmadi* further outline the duties of the *kotwal*. With help from the clerks he was required to make a list of all the houses and buildings in a city, town, or village that fell within his jurisdiction. He was also bound to take a census of all the residents in a *mohalla* (ward) and determine their professions and avocations. The *mir-i-mohalla* (headman) functioned as a spy and an informant. Upon leaving their houses the residents of a ward were required to inform the *mir-i-mohalla* and their neighbors so that they could prevent any possible thefts. The headman and the watchmen had the task of preventing unauthorized persons from entering the *mohalla*. The unauthorized persons had to be housed separately in an inn. They were also required to be vigilant against thieves and pickpockets. Upon the commission of a theft, they were required to produce the thief as well as the stolen property.

The Jaipur *Akhbarat* of 1668 records an incident where a Saiyyid and 20 Yusafzai Afghans rented a house in the capital. The people of the *mohalla* complained to the *kotwal* that although these persons were busy gambling during the day, at night they committed theft. These persons were arrested and locked up. During the inquiry they confessed that they had committed 24 thefts, and incriminating proof was also found against them. Emperor Aurangzeb determined that the 20 Yusufzai Afghans should be awarded capital punishment and the Saiyyid who was their accomplice was to be sent to the fort of Ranthambore as a prisoner (Jaipur Akhbarat, tenth year). The *kotwal* also had to be informed about the income and expenses of all the residents of the city and also kept information about those who were living beyond their means. If any person earned money from an irregular enterprise, the *kotwal* had to report the matter to the emperor. In order to prevent hoarding he was required to fix the prices of articles (Badauni 1976). The *mir-i-mohalla* was required to inform the *kotwal* regarding all marriages, feasts, births, and deaths that took place in the *mohalla*. Reliable informants were posted in the streets, bazaars, and on the fords of rivers in order to keep the *kotwal* informed about all significant events (Manucci 1966).

Functions and Duties of Faujdars

Though the *faujdar* was a government agent who was in charge of supervising the police of all villages in a region, his jurisdiction was so large that it rendered his authority ineffective. The *faujdar* had three main duties with respect to the punishment and prevention of acts of violence:

(a) Rebellions by local zamindars
(b) Organized raids by gangs of robbers
(c) Large-scale withholding of land revenue.

The *faujdar* was directly responsible for thefts that took place in his jurisdiction and was bound to compensate the party that had suffered the loss (Manucci 1966; see Fig. 5.2).

The role of the *faujdar* was generally limited to military ventures where there was large-scale violence or rebellion and it compelled him to deploy armed forces and take stringent action to crush the rebels. They were mainly responsible for maintaining law and order in the rural areas. Their jurisdiction was very large and could not assure strong and effective control of the miscreants and the outlaws. The *faujdars* were also personally responsible for crimes of theft. According to one account, Mr. Berber, an envoy to the Mughal emperor for the East India Company was robbed of Rs. 31,200. He demanded this money from the *faujdar* of Agra and made a representation about this theft to the Mughal court. The Emperor Aurangzeb ordered the *faujdar* to pay the envoy Rs. 15,000 as compensation and another Rs. 15,000 from the royal treasury since he had sustained physical injuries from the robbers (Sen 1949).

AREA	OFFICIAL
Subha	Subhedar
Sarkar	Faujdar
Pargana	Shikadar
Thana	Thanedar, Gumastha, Chaukidar, Qanungo, Barkandaz

Fig. 5.2 Provincial officials in Mughal India

Rural policing was left to the local *chowkidars* who were servants of the village community and were maintained by the villagers. They were not regarded as officers who were paid and supervised by the state. The Mughals left the villagers to govern their own affairs.

Besides the Faujdars and kotwals, the Mughals also employed an elaborate network of spies (Khufia-Navis) who corresponded directly with the imperial court. In an official *sanad* (decree) the Khufia-Navis is warned:

> Report the truth, lest the Emperor should learn the facts from another source and punish you. Your work is delicate; both sides have to be served …. In the wards of most of the high officers, forbidden things are done. If you report them truly, the officers will be disgraced. If you do not, you yourself will be undone (Sarkar 1972).

Application of Punishments

The Mughal rulers were Sunnis who belonged to the Hanafi School. They could not govern the country in strict observance of the law that was laid down in the fiqh manuals. As such the Muslim law was adapted to Indian conditions. The followers of any of the Sunnite Schools could adopt any one of the four jurists as their guide. However, the teachings of this jurist had to be followed consistently (Tyabji 1968). In Mughal India there were two very authoritative texts of this school; these are the *Fatawa Alamgiri*, and the *Hedaya* (Marghinani 1989). Both these texts were translated in the early nineteenth century (Hakeem 1998). Punishments were classified under three main categories: hadd, qisas, and taazir. However in its Indian environment three more types of punishment were added. These were banishment, incarceration, and *tashhir*.

The hadd punishment had three different goals: retribution, expiation, and general and specific deterrence. Mawardi (1989) delineated deterrence as the main justification for hadd punishments. Under Islamic criminal law six major offenses were recognized as hadd. Penalties for each of these offenses were prescribed in the Quran and the Sunna and enforced by the police.

In 1672 Emperor Aurangzeb issued a farman that to some extent supplemented Muslim theocratic law and in effect reduced some of its severity. According to the sharia, no punishment was meted out for theft of articles if their value did not reach the nisab (10 dirhams). This farman stipulated that if a person stole an article not worth 10 dirhams and for which he was not liable to hadd, she or he was to be verbally chastised in the first instance. Should the crime be repeated, taazir was meted out and she or he was to be kept in prison till she or he repented. Should the theft be committed a third time, the criminal was to be sentenced to life imprisonment or subject to execution. The stolen property was to be returned to the owner, or if the owner could not be found it was to be deposited in the *Bait-ul-Maal* (Mirat-I-Ahmadi I: 278, Khan 1965).

Qisas was prescribed under Islamic law for murder and personal injury. According to El-Awa (1984) the punishment for homicide under the sharia was of a dual nature. There are records of two cases of qisas that were dealt with by the authorities in Mughal India.

Adham Khan Atka v. Shams-ud-Din Atka (1562). Adham Khan murdered the prime minister, Shams-ud-din Mohammad Khan Atka. Adham Khan fell to the feet of the Emperor Akbar to beg forgiveness. Akbar punched him so hard in the face that he fell senseless. The Emperor then ordered that the culprit should be hurled headlong from the parapet. This was not sufficient to kill him. He was again thrown from the parapet. This eventually broke his neck and knocked his brains out Akbarnama (Beveridge 1989).

Jujhar Khan Bakshi v. Changez Khan (1573). Jujhar Khan Bakshi, an officer of Gujrat, slew Changez Khan. The mother of the deceased filed a complaint with Emperor Akbar while he was on a visit to Bharoach, Gujrat. After ordering a thorough enquiry into the matter, the charge was proved and the accused confessed his guilt. He was given capital punishment. The Emperor ordered him to be thrown under the feet of an elephant named Manmil; he was trampled in the presence of high and low Akbarnama (Beveridge 1989).

Taazir punishments were preventive and reformatory (Sarakhsi 1906). These punishments were not the only ones that could be administered in cases of Taazir. Any punishment that served the purpose of Taazir, that is, to prevent any further crime and reform the offender, could be used so long as it did not contradict the general principles of Islamic law (Ibn Farhun 1986). Besides determining the punishment, the ruler or qazi (judge) was also traditionally given the task of determining whether an act was criminal.

Al-Nafy: Banishment to Mecca, Bengal, or Bhakkar was another form of punishment in Mughal India. After the wars of succession Emperor Humayun punished both his brothers by ordering them to be sent as exiles to the holy city of Mecca (Sangar 1967). It is further recorded that Emperor Akbar punished one Haji Sultan for the offence of cow slaughter. As a consequence of the complaints made by the Hindus of Thanesar he was banished to Bhakkar.

The Mughals in India employed imprisonment liberally as a form of punishment. There were three prisons, which were located at Gwalior, Ranthambor, and Rohtas. Criminals condemned for life were sent to Ranthambor. They met their death about 2 months after they reached the prison. This prison was reserved for traitors who were first made to drink a huge amount of milk and then thrown off the steep and jagged cliffs (Sen 1949).

The Gwalior fort was a prison for the nobles while the Rohtas prison was used to house royal princes who had been condemned for life. The *qazis* were required to visit the prisons and inquire into the conditions of the prisoners, and also seek the release of those who exhibited signs of repentance. Orders for the release of prisoners were usually given on special occasions such as on the birth of a crown prince or recovery of the emperor from long illness. Thus the Akbarnama documents that on the birth of prince Salim, Emperor Akbar ordered that all the prisoners in the imperial dominions who had been imprisoned in the fortresses for long periods were to be released (Akbarnama, II: 345).

Temporary confinement was accomplished through police lock-ups. In the cities these were called *Chabutra-i-Kotwali*. There are frequent references to these in the newsletters of Aurangzeb. Guilty officers, thieves, and robbers were confined in these facilities. The *Mushrif* was in charge of the *Chabutra-i-Kotwali*. Persons could be released on bail if they could produce security. Thus the Akhbarat of 11-5-1694 records the fact that the zamindar of Deogarh, Bakht Buland, had been dismissed and locked up at the *Chabutra-i-Kotwali*. The Emperor ordered that if the accused was able to furnish a trustworthy surety, he could be removed from the *Chabutra-i-Kotwali* and handed over to Bahramand Khan and given an allowance of two rupees per day (Akhbarat-i-Darbar-i-Mualla, 11-5-1694).

Tashhir (shaming): The main purpose of this form of punishment was to degrade and shame the individual in a public venue so as to foster compliance with social norms. This type of punishment had its roots in the Institutes of Manu and was employed in ancient India. It continued to be used by the Mughals since it proved to be effective in the Indian setting. The most common form of this type of punishment was that a guilty person was mounted atop an ass and paraded through the streets. According to Manucci (1966) this punishment was inflicted on a woman who gave false information about a hidden treasure. The Prince (Shah Alam) ordered her robes to be torn to pieces. She was then mounted on an ass with her face towards its tail, and she was paraded throughout the city. After this degrading tour she was flogged before being released.

Dyarchy and the East India Company

Provincial Mughal administration was a miniature of that of the central government. The governor was also called nazim or subhedar. The administration was concentrated in the provincial capital. It was city government, where the government worked in the cities and was mainly concerned with inhabitants of the cities and the immediate neighborhood. The Mughals were essentially an urban people in India as also were their courtiers, officials, and the upper and middle classes of the Muslim population. Villages were neglected and despised and they dreaded village life as a form of punishment. The subhedar was officially referred to as the nazim or regulator of the province. His essential duties were to maintain law and order, help towards the smooth and successful collection of revenue, and execute the royal decrees and regulations sent to him.

Initial attempts at policing by the British in India commenced when the East India Company received the diwani (land grant) of Bengal, Bihar, and Orissa. The Emperor Shah Alam II issued a farman on August 12, 1765, which granted the East India Company these diwani rights for an annual tribute of 26 lakhs of rupees (26,00,000). Robert Clive, on behalf of the company pledged to pay this amount. Through this farman the company gained complete control over the financial affairs of these three provinces. However, the nawab was still responsible for the task of policing and the administration of criminal justice. This system of dual control or dyarchy had serious problems. The administration of criminal justice, especially policing, suffered. Through a combination of the craftiness of the English and neglect on the part of the nawabs, the English gradually encroached into and took control of the administration of criminal justice. The English became the de facto rulers of the eastern provinces during the tenure of Warren Hastings (1772–1785).

The East India Company felt that the ancient form of government should be preserved and the dignity of the nazim was maintained. Robert Clive introduced the notorious dual system which implied that the Company acquired real power but the nawab of Bengal was held legally responsible for the administration of criminal justice. The policy of dyarchy – rule of two – required the company's servants to adopt a policy of nonintervention in matters of justice and civil administration. In reality, however, the servants of the company were always interfering in the sphere of criminal justice. This policy of dyarchy, introduced by Clive failed badly. The zamindars who were responsible for maintaining peace and order neglected their duties. In fact the zamindars colluded with the criminal elements to steal from the populace. Under such conditions there was no stable administration and the region was plagued with chaos, instability, and disorder. To add further to this confusion, the English government ordered in 1770 that the institution of faujdars and amils was to be abolished. This in turn led these officials to join the ranks of the lawless and prey on the populace.

Warren Hastings realized the need to have a police force to reduce violent crime. He emphasized an indigenous system of policing. Civil and criminal (diwani and nizami) courts were established for each of the districts of Bengal in 1772 and the institution of the faujdars was restored in 1774. The zamindars were now required to assist the faujdars in the suppression of dacoities, violence, and disorder. The zamindars were warned of severe punishment if they failed to assist the faujdar and if their complicity with the criminal elements was discovered. Hastings tried to reform the police by creating a separate office under the direction of the president of the council to collect and coordinate information from the faujdars. According to Saha (1990), this office constitutes the germ from which the Indian police finally developed. Further changes were instituted in police administration in 1775 by Hastings: faujdari thanas were established in the main towns of the large districts. Each of these faujdari thanas was assisted by smaller police stations. The naib nazim was responsible for supervising police administration and a central police office was established in Murshidabad.

Though the Mughal form was preserved, this system did not have much substance and soon crumbled. The zamindars were jealous of the new power of the faujdars and as a consequence withheld their support. The faujdars were given a responsibility but this proved futile because they did not have the appropriate power or authority. In reality the faujdars were so weak that they needed protection for themselves. Even ordinary English servants did not hesitate to insult or assault the faujdars. As a consequence this institution of faujdari was abolished on April 6, 1781, except at Hooghli.

In the next phase of this experiment, the European judges of the diwani courts were given the power and responsibility of catching the public offenders and committing them with the darogas of the closest faujdari adalat (criminal court) with the stipulation that the charges had to be in writing. These judges also functioned as magistrates. Along with the magistrates, some of the zamindars were also authorized to arrest offenders with special permission of the governor general and council. Generally, the European judges, darogas, and zamindars had concurrent jurisdiction with respect to the police functions of the nizamat adalat. Hastings instituted further reforms by providing a number of watchmen and barkandazs to assist the European magistrates in discharging their police duties. These new reforms ushered in profound changes and succeeded in changing the predominantly military character of the faujdari system towards one that had a greater civilian bias.

A remembrancer of the criminal courts was also appointed to function from Fort William. This new official was expected to centralize the administration of criminal justice and co-ordinate the judicial and police functions. The magistrates and zamindars were required to submit monthly reports regarding the total number of persons arrested, tried, and convicted by the respective authorities to the remembrancer. A separate set of monthly reports was also required to be sent to the remembrancer by the faujdari adalats. These well-meaning reforms failed in practice. The legal complications proved to be a big stumbling block for an effective police system. Furthermore, the criminal courts under the nizamat adalat could not be steered away from following the divinely ordained sharia, which seemed to conflict with the English ideals of equity and justice. Hastings proved to be powerless with respect to modifying the existing law. His attempt to create a progressive police system turned out to be an exercise in futility. Violent crime, dacoities, and social disorder increased enormously on account of this half-baked policing.

When Cornwallis arrived in India in 1790, the administration of criminal justice was in utter disarray. Warren Hastings had preferred an indigenous police system, however, Cornwallis preferred a system where Europeans held control and responsibilities. As a consequence, Mohammad Reza Khan, the naib nazim, was removed from the sadar nizamat adalat and the court was shifted from Murshidabad to Calcutta. In future it was to be presided over by the governor.

According to Regulation XXII of 1793, radical changes were introduced into the police system. The police were now considered to be under the sole charge of officers of government who were specially appointed to that trust. A new institution of darogas was created. The zamindars were required to divest themselves totally of all police responsibilities and were ordered to disband their local police forces. The East India Company now directly took on the task of police administration.

Mughal Political Theory

The Mughal emperors, especially Akbar was responsible for secularizing the administration to a significant degree. By following the political theory of Abul Fazl and the premise of sulahkhul (universal tolerance) Akbar was able to create the foundation of a secular, multireligious, and multiethnic state. During this era, the political theory of Abul Fazl was based on Shia Islam. According to this theory, God had created a divine light that is passed down in an individual from generation to generation and this individual is the Imam. Imamate existed in the form of just rulers. The Imam as a just ruler had secret knowledge of God, was free from sin, and was responsible for spiritual guidance of humanity. This made the ruler superior to the sharia. Orthodox Islamic scholars opposed this political theory, but were co-opted into the government by a close partnership between the ulema and the emperor.

The next innovation introduced by Emperor Akbar was that all religions were equally tolerated in the administration of the state. The jiziya was repealed. Accordingly this theory of governance postulated the ruler's duty to ensure justice for all people in his care, irrespective of religion. It is on the basis of these political innovations that the Mughal rulers created an Islamicate model. The term *Islamicate* originally was defined by Hodgson (1979) as something that would refer not directly to the religion, Islam, itself, but to the social and cultural complex historically associated with Islam and Muslims, both among Muslims themselves and even when found among non-Muslims. The Mughals were able to integrate the elements of Indian and Islamic cultures and were thus able to create an Indo-Islamicate model of governance that was then pragmatically applied in order to bring peace, prosperity, and security for the subjects of the Mughals.

Implications of Mughal Policy

Even though the Mughals were Muslims they were able to apply a very tolerant and practical model of Islam and thereby govern India for almost 200 years. This chapter traces the administrative policy of the Mughals in India. The model of policing followed may be described as a centralized single model. Coming with a foreign system the Mughals adapted to the local conditions by incorporating some of the local practices and customs that proved to be effective in administering their subjects. The Mughals found it very difficult to go against local customs and traditions. The blend that ensued had its own unique administrative flavor. After the demise of the Mughal Empire its model of policing survived in most of the Mofussil areas of the country and was further built upon by the British. Though the legal system changed with the introduction of the Anglo-Saxon codes, the policing structure remained. The sharia system was eventually replaced by European codes in most of the former colonies. In India, the Indian Penal Code and the Code of Criminal Procedure, coupled with the Indian Evidence Act, finally replaced the Islamic system of criminal justice as the Muslim elites gradually lost power to the British.

References

Abul Fazl, I. M. (1993). *Akbarnamah*. Tihran: Muassassah-I-Mutalaat va Tahqiqat I-Farhangi.

Abul Fazl, Ibn Mubarak. (2010). *Ain-e-Akbari*. New York: General Books, LLC.

Akhbarat-I-Darbar-Mualla (Imperial Gazettes) of the Mughal government. November 1665 through 1707. The Jaipur State Archives, Jaipur.

Ali, Y. A. (1983). *The Holy Quran*. Brentwood: Amana Corp.

Alobeid, A. (1989). Police functions and organization in Saudi Arabia. *Police Studies, 10*, 80–84.

Araiz-o-farman (newsletters) from the imperial court dispatched by the representatives of the Princes, Rajas and Governors. 1681 through 1705.; The Raghubir Library, Sitamau.

Badauni, A. Q. (1976). *Muntakhab-ut-tawarikh*. Karachi: Karimsons.

Bayley, D. (1985). *Patterns of policing: A comparative international analysis*. New Brunswick: Rutgers University Press.

Bernier, F. (1891). *Travels in the Mogul Empire*. Whitefish: Kessinger Publishing, LLC.

Beveridge, H. (1989). *The Akbarnama of Abul Fazl*. Columbia, MO: South Asia Books.

El-Awa, M. S. (1984). *Punishment in Islamic law: A comparative study*. Indianapolis: American Trust Publications.

Griffiths, P. (1971). *To guard my people: The history of the Indian police*. Bombay: Allied Publishers.

Hakeem, F. (1998). From Sharia to Mens rea: Legal transition to the Raj. *International Journal of Comparative and Applied Criminal Justice, 22*(2), 211–224.

Hodgson, M. (1979). *The venture of Islam* (The classical age of Islam, Vol. 1). London: University of Chicago Press.

Ibn Farhun, Ibrahim ibn Ali. (1986). Tabsirat al-hukkam fi usul al-aqdiyah. Al-Qahirah: Maktabat al-kulliyat al-Azhariyah.

Khan, A. M. (1965). *Mirat-i-Ahmadi*. A Persian history of Gujarat (English translation) translated from the Persian original of Ali Muhammad Khan by M.F. Lokhandwala. Baroda: Oriental Institute.

Kurian, G. (1989). *World encyclopedia of police forces and penal systems*. New York: Facts on file.

Mandelslo, J. (1995). *Mandelslo's travels in Western India*. New Delhi: Asian Education Services.

Manucci, N. (1966). *Storia do Mogor* (Mogul India, 1653–1708) (William Irvine, Trans.). Calcutta: Editions India.

Marghinani, Ali ibn abi. (1989). The Hedaya: Commentary on the Islamic laws (Charles Hamilton, Trans.). Karachi: Darul Ishaat.

Mawardi, Ali bin Muhammad bin Habib. (1989). Al Ahkam al-Sultaniya. Cairo: al-Mansurah.

Mehta, J. L. (1986). *Advanced study in the history of medieval India*. New Delhi: Sterling.

Rao, S. V. (1967). *Facets of crime in India*. Bombay: Allied publishers.

Saha, B. P. (1990). *Indian police. Legacy and quest for formative role*. New York: Advent Books.

Sangar, S. P. (1967). *Crime and punishment in Mughal India*. Delhi: Sterling.

Sarakhsi, Muhammad bin Sahl (Abu Bakr). (1906). Kitab al-Mabsut. Cairo: Matbaat al-Saadah.

Sarkar, J. (1972). *Mughal administration*. Calcutta: Orient Longman.

Sen, S. N. (1949). *Indian travels of Thevenot and Careri*. New Delhi: National Archives of India.

Tavernier, J.-B. (1889). *Travels in India*. London/New York: Macmillan.

Tyabji, F. B. (1968). *Muslim law*. Bombay: N.M. Tripathi.

Chapter 6
Policing the Muslim Community in India

Introduction

The minorities are generally mistrusted and ill-treated by the police in almost every society. Research points to the tense relations that often exist between police and minorities in various nations (Hasisi 2008). Minorities also tend to be plagued by broken families, poor education, high residential density, low economic status, high levels of unemployment, and high adolescent dropout rates. Invariably, minority status results in negative perception among police officers that tend to profile them as criminals and undesirables. All this further results in higher rates of arrest and violence against them. In return, minorities lose confidence in the impartiality and legitimacy of the police (Tyler 2005). These variables suggest social disorganization among the minority community affecting their ability to compete with other groups in society. Moreover, the tense relationship with the police not only leads to the minorities being over-policed as suspects but also under-policed as victims (Hasisi 2008).

Police in modern societies use categories to solve pressing organizational problems and often use grossly inaccurate indicators to stigmatize a suspect segment of the population. In India, the Muslim community has been the other; suspected of extraterritorial loyalty and denigrated by the Hindu right, the community has been marginalized in the country. In particular, during situations of social conflict police tend to side with the Hindus, the majority community and in many instances even participate with anti-social elements targeting Muslims. Consequently, Muslims remain suspicious of the police and tend not to trust the officers. In everyday life too the police tend to profile Muslim youth as terrorists in extremist-affected areas or involved in organized criminal activities in other regions. It is therefore no surprise that the Muslims generally have low confidence in the Indian police and are unwilling to collaborate with them even when victimized. The mutual suspicion that exists between the police and minority communities has dangerous implications in this

F.B. Hakeem et al., *Policing Muslim Communities: Comparative International Context*,
DOI 10.1007/978-1-4614-3552-5_6, © Springer Science+Business Media New York 2012

case because of the size of community. Muslims number more than 150 million in India and form the third largest Islamic community in the world. Their alienation and perception of unequal treatment by the police have serious consequences for the country.

In this chapter I first examine the status and characteristics of the Muslim community in India and trace the history that has exacerbated its problems. I describe many examples where the Muslim community has suffered at the hands of police action or omission and explain some of the reactions flowing from this unfair treatment by state authorities. I also examine the nature and religious composition of policing in the country. This chapter argues that poor policing of the Muslim community may also be due to the internal problems of police administration. Some future trends and threats are assessed based upon the above arguments.

The Status of Muslims in India

The origins of the Muslim community in India can be traced back to the construction of first mosque built in 629 AD in Kerala by Arab traders (Najiullah 2006). Mohammad Bin Qasim's advent in 712 AD marks the forceful intrusion of Muslims to the Indian subcontinent that continued almost to 1761 when Ahmed Shah Abdali defeated the Marathas at the third battle of Panipat. From the twelfth century onwards, Muslim dynasties ruled major parts of India until the British gained control over the region. However, the expansion of the Muslim population in the region came from conversion; some by force but a good proportion comprising those seeking ways to escape the caste bondage in the Hindu system. By the end of British rule the Muslims constituted less than 25% of the people of South Asia. The partition of the country into India and Pakistan reduced the Muslim percentage in modern India down to 13.4% (2001 census) and to a vulnerable minority. The partition also created an extraordinary situation by opening a wide gulf with the Hindus who perceived Muslims to be the cause for division of the country and the uprooting of millions from what now constitutes Pakistan (and Bangladesh). The Muslim community began experiencing a sense of insecurity, frustration, and uncertainty out of independence and partition. The community also suffered the loss of its leaders, the majority of whom migrated to Pakistan. The dispute over Kashmir between the two nations has also kept the community hostage to religious identity and conflict with the Hindus.

There was considerable antipathy and suspicion of Muslims even among many of Nehru's cabinet colleagues and little was done to integrate the Muslims into the modern society being forged in independent India (Khalidi 2010). While assurances for a secular society and delinking of religion from governance were instituted in the constitution and maintained to a large extent efforts to assure Muslims of equal rights and opportunities in the new economy were generally neglected. The issues of poverty, education, and employment were rarely addressed while token actions to pacify Muslim sentiments were taken such as the ban on Salman Rushdie's book *The Satanic Verses*, subsidy for Haj pilgrimage, and grants for Muslim educational institutions. These issues, instead of accruing any substantial benefit to the Muslim community gave credence to the right-wing Hindu propaganda that the Congress government was appeasing the Muslims.

The continued neglect and indifference by various governments have reduced Muslims to an economic and educationally backward community. Literacy rates suggest that Muslims lag behind most communities in the country. The Census 2001 data given below describe this vividly.

Literacy rate among religious communities (in percentage)

Religious community	Literacy rate (female)	Literacy rate (all)
Muslims	50.1	59.1
Hindus	53.2	65.1
Christians	76.2	80.3
Sikhs	63.1	69.4
Jains	90.6	94.1
Buddhists	61.7	72.7

Source: Syed Shahabuddin in *Mainstream*, October 23, 2004: 14

The Muslim percentage in higher education is also very low. Muslims have fallen behind in terms of health access, employment, and representation in democratic elections. Lack of education has resulted in low employment in government services, particularly the police, army, and the bureaucracy. More significantly, Muslim women, already victim of economic and social backwardness have become even more vulnerable due to their faith-related issues. Muslim women are discouraged from working outside and have to be dependent upon the male members of the family. They enjoy few rights and can even be divorced over the telephone. While Bollywood and specific industries like leather, meat processing, and tailoring have a good representation of Muslims; in most other commercial activities the Muslims barely find employment. They face discrimination and are unable to compete with other communities to take advantage of the growing economy.

After persistent demands, the government of India appointed the Sachar Commission to examine the status of Muslims in India and its report presents some alarming data about this community (Sachar Commission 2006). The commission found that there is a general unease among the Muslims that relates to the question of their patriotism to the nation. They perceive on a daily basis that they have to prove their loyalty and provide evidence that they are not terrorists. "Muslims complained that they are constantly looked upon with a great degree of suspicion not only by certain sections of society but also by public institutions and governance structures. This has a depressing effect on their psyche" (Sachar Commission 2006: 11). Furthermore, buying or renting property of one's choice is becoming increasingly difficult for the Muslims. Apart from the reluctance of owners to rent/sell property to Muslims, several housing societies "dissuade" Muslims from locating there. Muslim identity also comes in the way of admitting children to good educational institutions. The commission also reports "for large number of Muslim women in India today, the only 'safe' space (both in terms of physical protection and in terms of protection of identity) is within the boundaries of home and community" (Sachar Commission 2006: 13).

The commission also found that insecurity is a general perception among the Muslims. Communal tensions and particularly instances of group violence instigate fear for their safety and security. The indifference of various governments towards taking action against such perpetuators and ensuring safety of the community has further pushed the Muslims into losing faith in the secular fabric of the country. The recurrent instances of deliberate violence directed at the community by specific political groups are radicalizing their members into retaliation. Furthermore, the Sachar Commission found that police and media tend to blame Muslims for instigating violence and usually do not come to their aid in times of crisis. However, the commission found that such perceptions vary across the nation. In many states ruled by leftist parties the Muslims evoked faith in the ability of the government to provide them security and unbiased action.

The commission came down heavily against the behavior of police agencies expressing concern over official apathy in dealing with Muslims. The commission stated that Muslims live with an inferiority complex as every bearded man is considered an ISI agent; whenever any incident occurs Muslim boys are picked up by the police and fake encounters are common. In fact, people complained that police presence in Muslim localities is more common than the presence of schools, industry, public hospitals and banks. Security personnel enter Muslim houses on the slightest pretext. The plight of Muslims living in border areas is even worse as they are treated as "foreigners" and are subjected to harassment by the police and administration (Sachar Commission 2006: 14). The commission added, "The lack of adequate Muslim presence in the police force accentuates this problem in almost all Indian states as it heightens the perceived sense of insecurity, especially in a communally sensitive situation."

The commission noted that Muslims are increasingly confining themselves into ghettos for fear of their safety, particularly in communally sensitive areas. "Ghettoisation, therefore, has multiple adverse effects: inadequacy of infrastructural facilities, shrinking common spaces where different sections can interact and reduction in livelihood options" (Sachar Commission 2006: 15). The experience of being a victim of discriminatory attitudes is high among Muslims, particularly among the youth. From poor civic amenities in Muslim localities, nonrepresentation in positions of political power and the bureaucracy, to police atrocities committed against them, the perception of being targeted for their religious identity is overpowering among a wide cross-section of Muslims. Besides, there is sensitivity that the sociocultural diversity of India is often not articulated in school textbooks (Khalidi 2010). Muslims are portrayed as barbarians, foreigners, and conquerors destroying Hindu temples.

Many of the problems enumerated in the earlier sections are not specific to Muslims; all the disadvantaged social groups face them. But the widespread sense of insecurity and the crisis of identity make Muslims perceive these problems as community-specific. However, the commission noted that "significant regional differences regarding the relative importance of identity, security and equity were however, evident across states" (Sachar Commission 2006: 25).

In 2004, the government of India formed another commission, The National Commission for Religious and Linguistic Minorities, with Supreme Court judge Ranganath Mishra as the Chairman. The objectives of the commission were to identify the socially and economically backward people among religious and linguistic minorities and recommend for them reservation and other development-oriented measures for educational and economic development. The commission's report has been placed in the Parliament with some delay and its recommendations for reservation in public jobs and educational institutes for the minorities have yet to be implemented. However, it is clear that both the Sachar and Misra Commissions have found the status of Muslims in India to be one of concern and have recommended positive action for their welfare.

The Muslim identity has come under attack by a variety of issues that have served to create a wedge between the Hindu and Muslim communities. The Bhartiya Janta Party (BJP), currently the main opposition party, has aggressively propagated that the Muslims do not practice family planning and that their population is increasing much faster than that of Hindus. A false scenario is projected that the Muslim population will take over the Hindu population in the near future and India will become part of Pakistan. The RSS ideologues have always argued for cultural nationalism as the positive nationalism of India. Golwalkar, the former chief of RSS too had seen culture, religion, and nation to be synonymous (Panikker 1993). There are many cultural practices that have a direct association with Hinduism and are still followed in government-sponsored events. The lighting of a lamp before beginning any conference, seminar, and even public meetings; the garlanding visitors, putting a "tikka" on the forehead and tying of rakhi are all practices that have been objected to by Muslim scholars who have dubbed them as the Hinduization agenda of the secular government (Khalidi 2010). The sum total of many prevailing customs, practices, and policies of the government have been seen as deliberate attempts to alienate the Muslims.

On a positive note, while the community is waiting for the government to address its problems there is evidence of realization that the Muslims themselves need to become proactive in tackling their problems. The renowned Muslim scholar, Asghar Ali Engineer (2000) writes,

It is dawning on Muslims that apart from preserving their Islamic identity they also have to carve out their niche in democratic secular India. Though still the emphasis is on building madrasas but more and more secular educational institutions are also coming up. More and more Muslims are realizing that girl education is also very important for their progress. A new middle class is also slowly coming into existence, which is increasingly championing the cause of modern education. Pressures are also building up from below for certain necessary changes in the status of women, particularly modification in the Shari'ah law as it operates in India.

A few days ago, Azim Premji, the richest Muslim and CEO of Wipro Corporation announced a gift of two billion (US) dollars for an educational trust in India (Chari 2010).

Communal Violence

After the bloody partition-related communal riots in 1947–1948, the country was at peace for almost a decade. However, a communal problem began manifesting itself with the attacks on Muslims in Jabalpur in 1962. After the demise of Nehru and weakening of the Congress government social conflict in several arenas began to raise its hood. Riots targeting the Muslims in Ahmadabad were followed by even more serious violence against the community at Bhiwandi in 1970. Serious violence against the Muslims took place in Jamshedpur, Bihar (1979), Varanasi (1977), Aligarh (1978), and Meerut (1987; all in UP) in which the partisan conduct of the police eroded the neutrality of the state (Engineer 2000).

But it was the inexperienced handling of the Shah Bano controversy and opening of the Ayodhya temple (Sharma 1999) to the Hindus that brought a new phase of confrontation between the two communities. Rajiv Gandhi succumbed to the pressure of Muslim leaders to overturn the Supreme Court judgment (AIR 1985) and passed the Muslim Women (Protection of Rights on Divorce) Act, 1986 permitting Muslims to be guided by their own religious laws. This appeasement was followed by another senseless act of opening the Ayodhya-based Babri Masjid and permitting Hindus to offer puja within the disputed structure. The BJP under the leadership of LK Advani stoked the controversy over the personal law for Muslims and launched the Ayodhya movement to not only escalate the Hindu Muslim tensions but also successfully mix religion into politics. "The temple campaign was religious only in form but political in content" (Panikker 1993: 63). The BJP made impressive electoral gains and came to power in four major states of the country. Finally, LK Advani, the BJP leader added fuel with his *Rath Yatra* (literally chariot journey) starting from Somnath and traveling all the way to Ayodhya to "liberate" the Ram temple. His Yatra was well supported by mass mobilization that sought to draw attention to the history of Muslim rulers' atrocities on the Hindus. A variety of symbolism was utilized to assert that Babri Masjid stands as a mark of humiliation of the Hindus at the hands of Muslims and thus must be destroyed. The powerful symbol of Ram, chariot, and special bricks inscribed with the name of Ram were used for Yagna (Hindu religious rituals). These bricks were wrapped in saffron clothes and displayed in a temple as "idols" of worship that aroused considerable religious frenzy. Women danced and sang *bhajans* (devotional songs) and processions were carried out in many parts of the country to bring Hindus on a common platform. Specially designed books, pamphlets, and posters were also used to arouse hatred for the Muslims and harp on Hindu unity. Advani's motorcade proved to be the "chariot of fire" instigating 116 communal acts of violence leading to the death of 564 people in every region of the country. The following table provides the gruesome statistics of his yatra.

States	No. of riots	No. killed
Andhra Pradesh	1	27
Assam	1	7
Bihar	8	19
Delhi	–	8
Gujarat	26	99
Karnataka	22	88
Kerala	2	3
Madhya Pradesh	5	21
Maharashtra	3	4
Rajasthan	13	52
Tamil Nadu	1	6
Tripura	1	–
Uttar Pradesh	28	224

Panikker (1993: 71)

The Ayodhya movement culminated in the destruction of the Babri Masjid on December 6, 1992 when a frenzied mob tore down the old structure. The BJP state government prevented the police from stopping the attack even though the strength of force was adequate to take action. The central government too was complicit in this wanton act of destruction for despite adequate intelligence the PM Narsimha Rao did not send the paramilitary forces to intervene. The Babri Masjid destruction provoked widespread agitation and attacks by the Muslims, particularly in neighboring Pakistan and Bangladesh that further aggravated the situation. The Shiv Sena used this conflict to unleash its wave of terror in Mumbai where a large segment of Muslims were targeted. This in turn led to the Mumbai underworld boss Dawood Ibrahim carrying out a major terrorist attack in the city that killed 257 people and wounded 713 (Forbes 2010). The major beneficiary of growing violence was the BJP that finally managed to capture Delhi from the Congress party and installing AB Vajpayee as the prime minister.

Another major riot took place in 2002 in Gujarat where Narendra Modi was the BJP chief minister. An attack by Muslims on Hindu pilgrims traveling in a train and burning of a coach at Godhra that killed 50 Hindus set off a major retaliation in which almost 2,000 Muslims were killed (Sinha 2010). These were organized attacks at the behest of the ruling BJP party in which the police were prevented from coming to the assistance of helpless Muslims. Again, the mobilization of the Hindus and communal tensions were used to political advantage by the BJP in Gujarat. Modi has not hesitated in linking the Indian Muslims as Pakistani agents through his "Mian Musharaff" terminology that apparently paid political dividends. He has won three elections so far and has been projected as the future prime minister in a BJP government. Even though he has little support outside Gujarat he symbolizes the apprehensions that Muslims feel in the country today.

Pakistan has skillfully exploited the situation in India by perpetuating terrorist attacks in various parts of the country. The Pakistan spy agency has spawned Muslim militant groups like Lashkar-e-Taiba (LeT), Hizb-ul-Mujahideen (HM), Harkat-ul-Mujahideen (HuM), Jaish-e-Mohammed (JeM), Jamiat-ul-Mujahideen (JUM), Harkat-ul-Jihad-al-Islami (HuJI), Jammu and Kashmir National Liberation Army, and many others to instigate terrorist attacks in India and to keep Kashmir on the boil (Satp.org 2010). Pakistan has also supported domestic extremists groups like underworld Don Dawood Ibrahim who carried out terrorist attacks in Mumbai in 1992 and the Student Islamic Movement of India (SIMI), which was accused of detonating nine bombs in Mumbai during the course of 2003, killing close to 80. The 2006 terrorist attacks on the Mumbai commuter-rail system that killed 183 people were also blamed on SIMI as well as the pro-Kashmir Pakistani terrorist group Lashkar-e-Taiba (LeT). The Mumbai attack on November 26, 2008 was another gruesome terrorist attack carried out by LeT and involving Pakistan's spy agency. Pakistan's direct involvement in major attacks on India is well documented (see Satp.org) and also known to the United States. According to Bob Woodward, "The ISI chief reportedly told the CIA less than a month after the attack that the terror strike was not an authorized operation but was carried out by rogue elements within the ISI" (cited in *India Today* 2010). Pakistan's continuing involvement in terrorist attacks on India has generally cast suspicion upon Indian Muslims and placed them in a precarious position.

However, the series of communal riots and particularly the killings in Gujarat riots have led many Muslim groups to adopt hard-line positions and call for revenge against the Hindus. Sikand (2003: 342) informs that

[I]n a letter sent to various Muslim leaders and Ulama, a top SIMI leader, "Abdul" Aziz Salafi insisted that the Muslims should make it clear to the government of India as well as to Hindu militants that the Muslims "would now refuse to sit low." He insisted that Muslims could no longer trust various "secular" parties to guarantee their rights and that they should now establish their own political identity.

It seems probable that Muslims pondering their fate in Hindu-nationalist-ruled India can only confirm their sense of isolation and impotence (Misra 2003), a reflection that is likely to push even moderate Muslims towards extremism.

On the other hand, the growing terrorist attacks in India carried out by Pakistan-based Islamic extremists have instigated the Hindus to form their own militias to attack Muslims and their shrines in India. The uncovering of the "Abhinav Bharat" group whose members have been linked to the RSS and the BJP is a pointer to the growing schism between the two communities (Haygunde 2008). This not only exacerbates the challenges of Indian police but furthers distrust and discontent when the police fail to find the killers or are unable to prevent terrorist attacks.

Muslim Presence in Indian Police

The ministry of home affairs that is the nodal agency for police services in India started providing information about Muslims serving in the various police services of different states and Union Territories from 2001 onwards. Such information has not been provided by any state governments and even today further details in terms of rankwise demographics is unavailable from official sources. To several queries made in the past the stock answer of the government has been that such information is not compiled within the uniform forces of the country. Perhaps due to the consistent demand for such information and the directives of the Sachar Commission this information of limited nature is now available from the *Crime in India* publication of the National Crime Records Bureau (2010). According to these data the Muslim percentage in state and UT cadre police forces vary from 0.2 in Mizoram to 57.9 in Jammu and Kashmir. In general, Muslims form barely a few percentage proportion of the total strength of the police force though in terms of numbers they go as high as 9,833 officers in Andhra Pradesh, a non-Muslim majority state. What could be termed as distressing is the fact that over the course of last 8 years, from 2001 to 2008 the number and percentage of Muslim representation in the police forces have generally declined. Using the base of the 2001 census it is clear that in no state except Jammu-Kashmir, do Muslims enjoy representation in the police in proportion to their numbers in the general population.

Appendix A, "Muslims in Police Forces," illustrates these trends. The table is somewhat misleading for there is missing information and counting procedures vary among the states. The data also do not provide a rankwide distribution and hence it is impossible to assert how many Muslims occupy supervisory positions in the police organization. There is no information available about Muslim representation in the paramilitary forces controlled by the central government. But from this table it seems that the states of Andhra Pradesh, Chattisgarh, Manipur, and Tripura have more Muslims than the corresponding proportion in the general population. Interestingly, Manipur-Tripura has just appointed a Muslim as the DGP of the state cadre too. Tamil Nadu had a proportionate percentage in 2001 data but this has gone down by 2008. Interestingly, the communist-ruled states of West Bengal and Kerala also have a smaller number of Muslims despite their proclamation of "secular credentials" and comparatively large Muslim population. Overall, it is clear that at the All India level Muslims, constituting 13.4% of the Indian population still constitute around 7% of the police personnel in the country. It must be kept in mind that state level numbers do little to reveal the deployment at the field levels where the proportions may vary considerably. It is unknown how many Muslims serve in the police stations where the community has a proportionately large presence. It is also unknown if in neighborhoods where communal tensions persist or where communal riots have taken place police deployment reflects the diversity of the people.

Information about the IPS cadre is more revealing as the home ministry provides the so-called "civil list" of all IPS officers serving in different states and organizations. There are 133 Muslims in the current IPS civil list out of a total of 3,262 officers in the country, a mere 4.07% of the total. While many states have a solitary Muslim officer, some like J and K have 29 and West Bengal has 12. In all the large states the percentage of Muslim IPS officers is much below the proportionate population in the state. On the other hand even with a single or two Muslim officers the following states, Chattisgarh, Himachal Pradesh, Nagaland, Punjab, and Sikkim have a higher percentage than the corresponding population figure.

What must be understood is that recruitment in the police and the army is merit based. For the subordinate ranks the selection begins with a physical test comprising running a mile, which has perforce to be done in open fields. It is difficult to discriminate anyone qualifying in these physical tests though nepotism and corruption do play a part at the final stage. Moreover, SP or above ranks do the selection and not every officer can be influenced across the country. The percentage of Muslims successfully qualifying in these tests is small. But this has more to do with their inability to compete with other communities than with official prejudice. The IPS selection is even more rigorous and extremely competitive. The brightest and highly qualified students of the best universities in the country compete for the limited number of positions within this service. Indeed, after a change in the examination system in the 1980s the number of students with professional degrees competing in the examination has increased substantially. At present almost half the officers serving in different ranks of the IPS have degrees ranging from engineering to medicine. The number of IPS officers who have graduated from prestigious institutes like the IITs and the IIMs is impressive to say the least. It is rare to find an IPS officer not having at least a postgraduate or doctoral degree. The Muslim community has not been able to take advantage of the educational opportunities of modern India and the numbers of Muslims going for higher education remains dismal. As such, they are unable to compete for the limited positions in the IPS. Furthermore, the IPS cadre allotment is a "lottery" system based upon vacancies, rank, and reserved categories of different states. Official policy or administrative bias does not determine the number of Muslim officers serving in a state, which creates problems of poor representation.

The varying percentages, though small, may suggest that different states treat Muslims differently. But the Muslim representation in the police appears to have little impact on their performance due to the politics of states. Thus, West Bengal and Kerala, historically ruled by communist parties, even with a low percentage of Muslims in police ranks have still successfully shielded the Muslim community from communal riots. On the other hand states like Bihar, UP, and Maharashtra have many Muslims in the police but these states have witnessed severe communal riots under partisan political parties. That police religious affiliation does not play such a major role in serving that community is perhaps best seen in the case of Delhi where Sikhs constitute a fair percentage of the police and yet in 1984 almost 3,000 Sikhs were killed by rampaging mobs. Similarly, Christian officers in Orissa have not been able to provide security to their community during the anti-Christian riots in 2008.

While it is apparent that Muslim representation in the police organization is much smaller than their proportion in the general population it is unclear how much discriminatory recruitment practices are responsible for this low representation. Most recruitment at the lower levels is simply based upon physical tests that are conducted openly. While allegations of corrupt practices in recruitment abound, successful and qualified Muslim candidates being turned away due to their religion is less heard of. It is well known that Muslims lag behind other communities in terms of education and that may be the significant factor in their failure to seek government employment. However, it could also be a factor that Muslims distrust the police and hence are reluctant to join it. Whatever may be the reasons Indian police in terms of demographics do not reflect the communities they serve and this is a factor in the poor image they have among the people.

Regional Impact of Religious Composition of the Police Forces

While there is no publicly available information about this subject some general information can be utilized to explore differences among various states in terms of the composition of the police and their treatment of the Muslim community. As seen in Appendix A, Muslim representation in the police forces is barely 10% in one or two states and almost negligible in many states. Virtual absence of Muslim police personnel has nevertheless not led to uniform discrimination of the minority group in the country. What is evident is the varied treatment across regions that are best explained in terms of the political composition of the ruling governments rather than composition of the police forces. The absence of communal riots in many parts of the country is equally noteworthy as their perpetuation in some other parts. While the BJP ruled Gujarat state witnessed one of the worst communal riots in 2002 (Engineer 2003), UP and Bihar provide examples of transformed police behavior coming from the change in political parties.

As mentioned above, serious riots against the Muslims took place under the Congress governments in the 1960s and 1970s in many parts of the country, particularly UP that has a large Muslim population. The Aligarh riots in 1978 marked a dark phase when the Provincial Armed Constabulary (PAC) allegedly participated in targeting the Muslims. The Meerut riots of 1982 further demonstrated that there was an institutional riot system (Brass 2006) that existed in many communally sensitive districts and which became operational to unleash violence. This essentially consisted of unruly urban lumpen proletariats who were mobilized and used by political parties to target Muslim businesses and people. However, with a change in political fortunes and rise of the backward castes the targeting of Muslims changed radically in these states. In 1992 while thousands of police officers stood guard at the Babri Masjid in Ayodhya and could have easily prevented the mob from destroying the old sixteenth century mosque, it was the decision of the BJP chief Minister Kalyan Singh and other top BJP party functionaries that prevailed and stopped the police from taking action. After the Babri Masjid demolition a change in political fortunes took place with the rise of Samajwadi party under Mulayum Singh Yadav and then Bhajun Samaj Party under Mayawati. These two politicians and their parties sought to win the support of the Muslims and in return prevented any communal violence in the last 15 years. The issues of Ayodhya, Varanasi, and Mathura, high on the Hindutava agenda remain present and strong in this state. The memories of PAC targeting Muslims in Aligarh and Meerut and religious composition within the police remaining skewed against the minority community, the police have functioned differently and provided protection to the Muslims.

The situation in Bihar has been similar. In 1989 a deadly riot took place at Bhagalpur where reportedly 2,000 Muslims were killed (Engineer 1995). However, once Lallo Yadav took command he forged a coalition with the Muslim groups and ensured that no violence directed at the Muslims took place. His determination to arrest LK Advani who was on his Rath Yatra to "liberate" Ayodhya also established his credentials as a "secular" politician and support of the Muslims. The same police force that failed to provide security to the Muslims at Bhagalpur has stood by them ever since and acted without prejudice. Interestingly, even when Lallo was replaced by JD(U) party chief Nitish Kumar who formed a coalition government with the BJP, the situation did not change. Nitish Kumar too kept the BJP in check and did not allow Narendra Modi, the controversial chief minister of Gujarat to visit his state. These symbolic and practical steps ensured his recent victory in the state assembly elections where he secured a thumping majority.

On the other hand BJP-ruled states like Gujarat saw Modi use the communal card to full advantage and win three elections in a row by his venomous tirade against the Muslim community. Even today, inquiry into the Gujarat riots in which several senior BJP ministers are involved is not proceeding properly due to the interference by the state functionaries. The involvement of many senior IPS officers in working at the behest of BJP politicians and killing Muslims in staged encounters is under investigation by the CBI. Perhaps the lessons of Gujarat were learned for when BJP assumed power in Rajasthan and MP it did work to prevent any communal incident in the state. While there is hardly any Muslim representation in the police forces of these two states violence against Muslims has been negligible.

In Maharashtra, BJP along with the rabid Shiv Sena party has continued to target the Muslims till it lost power in the beginning of the new millennium. In the early part of the 1990s the Shiv Sena perpetuated serious riots against the Muslims. The Justice Sri Krishna Commission found considerable evidence of collusion between the politicians and the police in instigating this violence. The commission castigated the police personnel for their communal stance in the discharge of duties:

> The response of police to appeals from desperate victims, particularly Muslims, was cynical and utterly indifferent. On occasions, the response was that they were unable to leave the appointed post; on others, the attitude was that one Muslim killed was one Muslim less …. Police officers and men, particularly at the junior level, appeared to have an in-built bias against the Muslims which was evident in their treatment of the suspected Muslims and Muslim victims of riots. The treatment given was harsh and brutal and, on occasions, bordering on the inhuman …. The bias of policemen was seen in the active connivance of police constables with the rioting Hindu mobs, on occasions, with their adopting the role of passive on-lookers on occasions, and, finally, their lack of enthusiasm in registering offenses against Hindus even when the accused was clearly identified and post-haste classifying the cases in "A" (True but not detected) summary.
>
> *Report of the Justice B.N. Srikrishna Commission on the Mumbai riots of 1992–1993*
>
> Cited in Indianmuslim.com

Unfortunately, little action has been taken about its recommendations. The change in politics and replacement by the Congress and NCP combine has brought some peace to the beleaguered state. Even the major terrorist attack launched from Pakistan on 26/11 in 2008 did not provoke a communal backlash and the government has been able to control violence directed against the Muslims. The BJP-supported extremists have also been checked by the arrest of Abhinav Bharat members in attacking Muslims at Malegaon (CNN-IBN 2008). This investigation is continuing and the police are working independently to take action against those attacking the Muslims.

Similarly, Andhra Pradesh has also seen political prudence in seeking the support of the Muslims. Even though BJP instigated serious violence in the early 1990s at Hyderabad but the government of Chandra Babu Naidu ensured that police act independently against the perpetuators. This could come about even when his party was aligned with the BJP at the Center. At present, the Congress party is back in power and has worked to keep Muslim support.

Surprisingly, in communist-ruled Kerala there is a reversal of the situation. The Muslims, who constitute almost 23% of the population and are in a majority in several districts enacted serious violence against the Hindus. In Kozikode district nine Hindus were killed in a single act of violence by a Muslim mob (Indian Express 2003). Fortunately, the police have acted professionally there and have been taking action against the offenders. But in a bizarre case a Muslim gang hacked off the wrist of a Christian teacher who allegedly asked some questions about the Prophet in the college examination (Selvan 2010). While the offenders have been arrested the Christian community has not supported the teacher that appears to have diffused the confrontation between the two communities.

It is relevant to point out that recently the BJP activists have targeted the Christians who they accuse of conversion. Violence against the Christians took place in Gujarat, MP, and to a large scale in Orissa (Chatterjee 2009). Perhaps these induced the CM Naveen Patnaik to sever relations with the BJP and freely take action against the culprits. In the NorthEastern states, particularly Assam, where large-scale violence against the "Bangladesh migrants" occurred in the 1980s the situation has simmered down. Police are battling ULFA, a terrorist group and other insurgencies, a battle that has taken eyes off the communal problem. Of course, the situation in J and K remains grim. The separatist call of Azadi (freedom) has been escalated in recent years despite two clean elections and rise of regional parties. However, J and K remains the single state with a majority of Muslims in the police force and this has not affected their performance in taking action against those violating the curfew or indulging in violence.

Even when Muslim representation remains low, the political decision to seek out their support ensures that the police serve the community without discrimination. Many Muslim IPS officers have been assigned important positions in the administration. Even in Gujarat, Narendra Modi has posted SHS Khandwawala, a Bohra Muslim as DGP of his state. That political consideration is the guiding factor in peacekeeping was best seen when the controversial Ayodhya judgment came about this year in November. There was considerable apprehension regarding the verdict of the court and its impact upon political developments in the country. However, a firm commitment by the non-BJP ruling parties and a sense of realism on part of the BJP too, saw massive mobilization and directions to the police to prevent any kind of a backlash (Madhusoodan 2010). Despite the controversial judgment in which the court essentially accepted BJP's plea of land belonging to the Hindus (Varadarajan 2010), no violence took place. The political decision rather than any other factor, including low Muslim representation is the *raison d'etre* for the good or biased performance of the police forces.

The above examples suggest that rather than the composition of the force in terms of religious affiliation it is the political objectives that determine police behavior. Even where the police earlier suspected the Muslims, like UP and Bihar, a change in political leadership forced a change in behavior of the force. Both West Bengal and Kerala where the communist parties have been in power for a long period of time, the police have acted to prevent communal tension and worked to provide security to the minority community. While the police have acted brutally in many of these states, their actions have been directed against the "naxalites" and their supporters. The police role is politically determined and controlled. Many of the above-mentioned riots occurred because politicians played a major role in preventing police action against the perpetuators. On the other hand, with a change of political parties the same officers do act to prevent communal violence.

Role of Police Leadership in Addressing Muslim Grievances

Sadly, politicization has affected many police personnel who actively support political objectives by omission or even direct action against the Muslim community. The rot has set in the ranks of senior police leadership also where a good number of IPS officers have disgraced themselves by violating their oath and acting dishonorably. Several IPS officers are either in prison or facing inquiries into their role at the behest of politicians. Three IPS officers are facing murder charges for killing some Muslims (and Hindus) as alleged terrorists (Rediff News 2007). The police commissioners of Ahmadabad and Mumbai have been charged for not using the force at their command to stop violence against the Muslims. Many IPS officers have joined political parties and contested elections after their retirement. In many states IPS officers are known to be aligned with one or the other political party and to misuse their powers to further political objectives.

However, the majority of the police force and the leadership are professional and follow due process. The efforts to recruit Muslims into the police force are a constant endeavor. Recruiters visit Aligarh Muslim University and other institutions, engage civic groups, and hold special drives to bring some diversity into the force. An enterprising IPS officer has opened a special instructional center to assist Muslims in competing for engineering examinations (Khan 2008).

The police have also been carrying out a large number of special operations to provide security to the Muslims and vulnerable communities. During the festive seasons, particularly when the Hindu and Muslim festivals fall together the police invariably engage the Muslim representatives to build confidence and provide adequate security to the community. Since Muslim police personnel are generally few in numbers they invariably get good field postings. These are not token measures but a way to build confidence in the community. The numbers of IPS officers who have attained the highest rank of DGP of the state is also fairly high. In Bihar, there have been three such chiefs of police in the past two decades and the post of home secretary has also gone to Muslim IAS officers. As mentioned, a Muslim IPS officer has been posted as the DGP of Gujarat state by Modi despite his known antagonistic attitude towards the Muslims. Perhaps, Muslim presence in the intelligence agencies is deliberately very low but nevertheless, Muslim IPS officers do occupy senior positions in most state and central government forces.

A number of innovative initiatives have been undertaken by police officers to address the problems of different communities including the Muslims. Suresh Khopade, a well-known police officer of the Maharashtra cadre earned praise for safeguarding Bhiwandi during the 1992 communal tensions. Analyzing the data from the previous riots he realized that Hindu Muslim communities are generally segregated and lack of communication between them helps spread rumors. These are used by the anti-social elements to take advantage of the situation and instigate violence (Khopade 2003). Accordingly, he formed around 70 "Mohalla Committees" in the district that comprised 50 Hindus and 50 Muslims of the same neighborhood. A subinspector was put in charge of this committee that was required to meet once every 15 days and act as a liaison between the residents and the local police. The committee provided the police with important intelligence about anti-social elements and helped curb rumors. Furthermore, it was empowered to address small petty disputes among the residents. Most significantly it helped bring attitudinal changes among the police personnel who developed a close association with the associations (Mitra 2006). The results were encouraging; during the Babri Masjid-related communal riots that engulfed Mumbai and most parts of the country, Bhiwandi remained peaceful. This experiment of Mohalla Committee has been replicated in many other parts of India under different names and has achieved success in addressing the problems of communal conflict by promoting civic engagement between the two communities (Varshney 2002). The Mumbai police too have embarked on a major initiative of engaging the citizens as coproducers of their own safety and given shape to what has come to be known as *mohalla ekta* (literally neighborhood unity) committees that have played an important role in maintaining peace in difficult situations (Thakkar 2004).

The southern states have taken a number of pioneering initiatives to bridge the police community gap and also develop mechanisms to provide protection to the minorities. A decentralized and personalized policing approach was undertaken by Andhra Pradesh police under the scheme of "Maitri" that sought to work with the people and maintain peace in the community. The Kerala police have launched a major community-policing initiative called "Janamaithri Suraksha" seeking co-operation from the citizens to address local issues (Sandhya 2010). These community-policing projects have also helped bridge the suspicion between the two communities and establish peace in the region. The "Friends of Police" movement in Tamil Nadu (Phillip 2006) is another major project that has brought in more than a million people to enroll with the police to assist in addressing local problems. Under the stewardship of Police Commissioner RadhaKrishanan, a "Samarth Yojna" community-policing project was launched in Coimbatore city of Tamil Nadu where communal riots had occurred. Under this project "area committees" were formed that empowered the citizens to work with the police in sharing intelligence and reducing communal feelings. A similar project was undertaken in Trichur city under the guidance of Superintendent of Police Tripathy that helped establish peace between the two factions (CHRI 2010).

Such schemes and ways of reaching out to the citizens and providing a sense of security to the minorities and vulnerable groups have been undertaken in other regions of the country too. Assam police have launched the "Prahari" scheme to bring together various sections of society and bridge the gap with the police. A similar project under the name of "Aaswas" has been functioning to address the issues of violence and terrorism in the region. The Himachal Pradesh police have started community policing projects to mobilize the people and involve them in crime prevention, maintenance of law-order, and to provide the police with local intelligence to keep surveillance over groups instigating communal conflict. Zahur Zaidi, a senior IPS officer produced a short documentary film titled *Aap aur Hum* (*You and Me*) to inform citizens about their rights and responsibilities (CHRI 2010). Sahayata (help) is a community-policing project in the Nadia district of West Bengal to provide counseling and resolve local disputes amongst different sections of the society.

Wherever and whenever the police leadership could function independently the results have been encouraging. Unfortunately, political control over the police has meant that police have also operated to serve political objectives. For some of the political parties discrimination against the Muslims is a basic ideology and seen as a way to build political capital. There is enough evidence to suggest that the BJP and Shiv Sena have used the police to discriminate and perpetuate violence against the Muslims. In the fractured democratic polity of the country such elements do find the space to implement their dangerous agenda.

Limitations of Police to Address Minority Concerns

But failures in the handling of communal violence also stem from large systematic problems in the Indian police. First, the nature of Indian society is reflected in the police forces too. Most officers are deeply religious, follow caste traditions, are divided over regional identities, and subscribe to a patriarchical elitist society. It is also a common observance that police brutality is more likely in highly unequal societies and in those where particular racial, ethnic, religious, and linguistic minorities are excluded from full participation. All states draw boundaries that define rights to membership and lay down criteria for denying participation and benefits to some groups, particularly minorities. In India, Muslims are generally unwelcome in many spheres of life. Many Hindus would not rent their apartments on grounds that Muslims eat beef and their nonvegetarian diet will "pollute" religious practices. For others, segregation of women and involvement in leather processing industries is also a factor to deny space in their homes. Unfortunately, police personnel share these perceptions too and this affects their behavior towards the Muslims.

The organizational problems affecting police performance are also deep rooted. The police have been designed as a colonial force to serve the interests of the rulers. Not much has changed in terms of structure, culture, and functioning from 1861 when the British through the Police Act of 1861 shaped the police. The police are not designed to be answerable to the people (Arnold 1992) except through an indirect authority of the home minister, who as an elected representative holds the police accountable on behalf of the people. This undiluted responsibility is "too broad to afford relief to the people who have no access to the channels of power" (GOI 1981: LXI 61.1). The other mechanisms of accountability are through the courts to which the police are beholden for their actions. Even though courts have passed severe strictures against police officers, yet the courts have not been able to force the department to follow the law closely. The only mechanism that sometimes works is the system of organizational accountability wherein senior officers evaluate and control the performance of the subordinate officers. Thus, it is only the elitist IPS police leadership (Verma 2001) that occasionally succeeds in redressing public grievances. However, an IPS officer is too remote an authority for the majority of the poor and illiterate people to approach directly. The reputation of most of the subordinate officers remains such that they inspire little faith among the people.

Thus, people are forced to approach the local politicians to intervene on their behalf in matters concerning the police organization. The local politicians, Zila Parishad members, MLAs, MPs, as the people's representative, howsoever corrupt and self-seeking they may appear to be, do play a role in solving people's problems by taking public grievances to the police. Unfortunately, the IPS leadership has been unwilling to accept a role for the politicians in police administration. They resent such interventions by the politicians and dub it as interference in their responsibilities. For many citizens, the politician is the only person who can force the police officers to do something. In such a situation, the Muslims are at a disadvantage. The proportion of Muslims getting elected and garnering power over the governing apparatus is small. The problems of the Muslim community are not addressed due to the lack of political power wielded by the community leaders. In contrast, positive discrimination policies and reservations in elected bodies have meant that the scheduled castes and tribes have political leaders who can be approached to force the police to take necessary action.

Furthermore, the armed police model is the prevailing mode of functioning and deliberately, the personnel are kept away from the people they serve. The police are required to stay in barracks and can serve only a short time at any one post. This hinders building rapport with the community and understanding their problems. Outdated operational practices also hinder efficient performance and lead to bureaucratic obstruction. For instance, the citizen complaint is registered under the provision of Section 154 CrPC that leaves considerable discretion in the hands of stationhouse officers. Consequently, people find it difficult to register their complaints and have to bribe officers or approach some intermediary for the purpose. The ad hoc discretionary system of complaint registration has played havoc with the crime statistics. Not only are these extremely unreliable but also for ages have been "managed" to keep the authorities satisfied. The criminal justice data in India has been historically unreliable and tends to suggest organizational practices rather than a reliable account of criminality and its control mechanism in the country. Gurr et al. (1977) in their detailed analysis of crime in the metropolitan city of Calcutta found that police statistics are managed to present satisfactory performance of the police rather than the ground situation. In periods of turmoil when major conflicts broke out in the city these statistics show downward trends in contrast to what was happening in society. Although *Crime in India* has been published since 1953 the official data are poorly recorded and presented. The National Crime Records Bureau is responsible for collecting crime-related data but is it dependent upon the state police forces for providing them with the statistics. Most state units treat this exercise with disdain. The discrepancy in cases of juvenile delinquency stands out as an illustrative example. In the year 2004, the state of West Bengal reported just four cases, which was less than the numbers for Goa, and sparsely populated Arunachal Pradesh, for the same year. It is inconceivable that the metropolitan city of Kolkata with a population of 14 million plus would have only two cases of juvenile delinquency. Either the region has little saints or else the police figures were totally incorrect (Verma 2005). Yet, little attention is ever given to such fictional statistics and no attempt appears to be made to take corrective measures.

Epilogue

The consequences for police management (and the country) from such practices are serious. First, the Indian police have become indifferent towards an empirical evaluation of their performance. Impression and utility to the political rulers constitute the basis for posting, transfer, and promotion of officers in every state. Second, preventive measures and deployment of personnel are done on an ad hoc basis rather than sound policies driven by empirical data analysis. Third, the demands for counting Muslims in the armed forces have been denied on specious grounds and even though it is well understood that the minorities are estranged, little systematic effort is undertaken to address this problem. Although it is well understood that Muslims face serious problems and that the police role in addressing their grievances needs a major change there is still little information and data to understand this properly.

It remains clear that the alienation of Muslims must be removed and for this the police need not only to open its doors for greater recruitment but also to address their specific problems. Research has consistently demonstrated that public confidence in the justice system is determined, in large part, by trust in police (Sivasubramaniam and Delahunty 2008). When citizens trust police, they are more likely to perceive police authority as legitimate, and thus more likely to cooperate with authorities and comply with the law (Sunshine and Tyler 2003). Trust in the police is linked to the ability of police officers to provide basic citizen security (Goldsmith 2003). Therefore, factors that promote or inhibit Muslims' trust in the police warrant special attention by Indian authorities.

Abbreviations and Unfamiliar Terms

BJP	Bhartiya Janata Party, a right-wing political party
CrPC	Code of criminal procedure
DGP	Director General of Police, the highest police rank in the state
Hindutava	A term used to symbolize the political objectives garbed in terms of Hindu religion
IIM	Indian Institute of Management
IIT	Indian Institute of Technology
ISI	Inter-Services Intelligence, Pakistan-based spy agency
JD(U)	Janata Dal-United, a political party
MLA	Member of legislative assembly
Mohalla	Neighborhood
MP	Member of parliament
Naxalites	Left-wing extremist groups operating in Central India
NCP	Nationalist Congress Party
Rakhi	A thread tied on the wrists symbolizing affection between brother and sister
RSS	Rastriya Swayam-Sewak Sangha, a militant Hindu organization
Tikka	Religious mark on the forehead used by many chaste Hindus
Ulama	Muslim cleric
ULFA	United Liberation Front of Asom, an extremist group operating in Assam
Zila Parishad	District Council

References

All India Reporter. (1985). Supreme Court 945, Vol. 72, part 859-July, *Mohd Ahmed Khan, Appellant vs Shah Bano Begum and others, Respondents* (from Madhya Pradesh).

Arnold, D. (1992). Police power and the demise of British rule in India 1930–47. In D. M. Anderson & D. Killingray (Eds.), *Policing and decolonisation* (pp. 42–61). Manchester: Manchester University Press.

Brass, P. R. (2006). *Forms of collective violence: Riots, pogroms and genocide in Modern India.* Gurgaon: Three Essays Collective.

Chari, S. (2010). Azim Premji makes Rs. 8,846 crore gift, *Livemint.com*, Dec 1. http://www.livemint.com/2010/12/01232953/Azim-Premji-makes-Rs8846-cror.html. Accessed 6 Dec 2010.

Chatterjee, A. (2009). *Violent gods: Hindu nationalism in India's present; narratives from Orissa.* Gurgaon: Three Essays Collective.

CNN-IBN. (2008). *Hindu groups linked to terror, Parliament rocked*, Oct 23. http://ibnlive.in.com/news/hindu-groups-linked-to-terror-parliament-rocked/76543-3.html. Accessed 29 Nov 2010.

Commonwealth Human Rights Initiative. (2010). *Community policing experiments/outreach programs in India.* www.humanrightsinitiative.org/.../community_policing_experiments_in_india.pdf. Accessed 24 Nov 2010.

Engineer, A. A. (1995). Bhagalpur riot inquiry commission report. *Economic and Political Weekly*, 15 July 1995, pp. 1729–1731. Bombay: Sameeksha Publications.

Engineer, A. A. (2000). *Islam and Muslims of India: Problems of identity and existence*, Indian Muslim, Dec 16–31. http://www.indianmuslims.info/articles/asghar_ali_engineer/islam_and_muslims_in_india_problem_of_identity_and_existence.html. Accessed 27 Nov 2010.

Engineer, A. A. (2003). *The Gujarat carnage.* Mumbai: Orient Longman.

Forbes. (2010). *Powerful people: November 2010 – Dawood Ibrahim Kaskar.* http://www.forbes. com/profile/dawood-ibrahim-kaskar. Accessed 27 Nov 2010.

Goldsmith, A. (2003). Policing weak states: Citizen safety and state responsibility. *Policing and Society, 13,* 3–21. http://www.dnaindia.com/bangalore/interview_we-will-involve-people-to-ensure-peace-on-friday_1440867. Accessed 29 Nov 2010.

Government of India. (1981). Report VIII of the National Police Commission. New Delhi: Ministry of Home Affairs.

Gurr, T. R., Grabosky, P. N., & Hula, R. C. (1977). *The politics of crime and conflict: A comparative history of four cities.* London: Sage.

Hasisi, B. (2008). Criminology: Police, politics and culture in a deeply divided society. *The Journal of Criminal Law and Criminology, 98*(3), 1119–1145.

Haygunde, C. (2008). Abhinav Bharat was hijacked by outsiders- Probe, *ExpressIndia.com,* Nov 2. http://www.expressindia.com/latest-news/abhinav-bharat-was-hijacked-by-hardliners-probe/380249/. Accessed 5 Dec 2010.

India Today. (2010). ISI chief admits role in 26/11, *Indiatoday.in,* Sept 28. http://indiatoday.intoday. in/site/Story/114248/113/mumbai-two-terrorists-on-loose-.html. Accessed 2 Dec 2010.

Indian Express. (2003). *Seven die in Kerala communal violence,* May 3. http://www.indianexpress. com/oldStory/23185/. Accessed 29 Nov 2010.

Khalidi, O. (2010). *Khaki and ethnic violence in India: Armed Forces, Police and ParaMilitary during communal riots* (2nd ed.). Gurgaon: Three Essays Collective.

Khan, I. (2008). *Now super 30 like IIT coaching for poor Muslims.* http://www.thaindian.com/ newsportal/uncategorized/now-super-30-like-iit-coaching-for-poor-muslims_10059217.html. Accessed 25 Nov 2010.

Khopade, S. (2003). *Navi Disha- Police Prashasanachi Navi Disha.* Mumbai: Sneh Prakashan (in Marathi language).

Madhusoodan, M. K. (2010). We will involve people to ensure peace on Friday'. DNAIndia.com, 21 Sept (Tuesday).

Misra, P. (2003). India's time of Reckoning. *New Statesman* 29 Sept.

Mitra, S. K. (2006). *The puzzle of India's governance: Culture, context and comparative theory.* London: Routledge.

Najiullah, S. (2006). The status of Muslims in India, *Indianmuslims.com,* Apr 21. http://www.indian-muslims.info/statistics/articles_related_to_statistics/syed_najiullah_the_status_of_muslims_in_ india.html. Accessed 22 Nov 2010.

National Crime Records Bureau. (2010). *Crime in India 2008.* Faridabad: Government of India Press.

Panikker, K. N. (1993). Religious symbols and political mobilization: The agitation for a Mandir at Ayodhya. *Social Scientist, 21*(7–8), 63–78.

Phillip, P. V. (2006). *Friends of police movement: A roadmap for proactive people protection.* Hyderabad: ICFAI University press.

Rediff News. (2007). *3 IPS officials arrested for fake encounter,* Apr 24. http://www.rediff.com/ news/2007/apr/24ips.htm. Accessed 2 Dec 2010.

Sachar Commission. (2006). *Socio, economic and educational status of the Muslim community in India: A report.* New Delhi: Government of India.

Sandhya, B. (2010). Community policing initiatives in Kerala. *The Hindu,* 9 Nov.

Satp.org. (2010) Pakistan terrorist groups. *South Asia Terrorism Portal.*

Selvan, P. (2010). Muslims cut off the hand of a Christian blasphemer in Kerala, *Sulekha.com.* http://forums.sulekha.com/forums/coffeehouse/muslims-cut-off-the-hand-of-a-christian-blas-phemer-in-kerala-1037637.htm. Accessed 29 Nov 2010.

Sharma, R. S. (1999). *Communal history and Rama's Ayodhya* (2nd ed.). Delhi: People's Publishing House (PPH), Revised Edition.

Sikand, Y. (2003). Islamist assertion in contemporary India: The case of the students Islamic movement of India. *Journal of Muslim Minority Affairs, 23*(2), 335–346.

Sinha, M. (2010). Bringing violence perpetuators to justice: Experiences and prospects – case of Gujarat. Paper presented at the *Group Violence, Terrorism and impunity: Challenges to Secularism and Rule of Law in India: A Workshop*, Boston: MIT, 9–10 Apr 2010.

Sivasubramaniam, D., & Goodman-Delahunty, J. (2008). Ethnicity and trust: Perceptions of police bias. *International Journal of Police Science and Management, 10*(4), 388–401.

Sunshine, J., & Tyler, T. R. (2003). The role of procedural justice and legitimacy in shaping public support for policing. *Law and Society Review, 37*(3), 513–548.

Thakkar, U. (2004). Mohalla committees of Mumbai: Candles in ominous darkness. *Economic and Political Weekly*, 7 Feb 2004.

Tyler, T. R. (2005). Policing in black and white: Ethnic group differences in trust and confidence in the police. *Police Quarterly, 8*, 322–342.

Varadarajan, S. (2010). Force of faith trumps law and reason in Ayodhya case, *The Hindu*, Oct 1. http://www.thehindu.com/news/national/article805124.ece?homepage=true. Accessed 22 Nov 2010.

Varshney, A. (2002). *Ethnic conflict and civic life: Hindus and Muslims in India*. New Delhi: Oxford University Press.

Verma, A. (2001). Making of the police manager: Bharat versus India. *International Journal of Comparative Criminology, 1*(1), 77–94.

Verma, A. (2005). *Indian police: A critical evaluation*. Delhi: Regency.

Appendix A: Muslims in Police Services

States/ Uts	# Muslims 2001	% Muslims 2001	# Muslims 2008	% Muslims 2008	% Pop of Muslims 2001 Census
ANDHRA PRADESH	9610	12.3	9833	12.1	8.4
ARUNACHAL PRADESH	63	1.2	85	1.2	1.9
ASSAM	8061	15.1	2284	4.4	30.9
BIHAR	3186	7.0	2712	4.5	13.3
CHHATTISGARH	1133	9.3	889	2.6	2.0
GOA	67	1.8	69	1.5	6.8
GUJARAT	3813	6.3	3097	5.3	9.1
HARYANA	837	2.6	256	0.6	5.8
HIMACHAL PRADESH	188	1.5	187	1.4	2.0
JAMMU & KASHMIR	32588	55.2	36910	57.9	67.0
JHARKHAND	NR		1597	3.1	13.8
KARNATAKA	4195	8.3	3960	5.3	12.2
KERALA	4898	11.3	5914	14.4	24.7
MADHYA PRADESH	3090	3.2			6.4
MAHARASHTRA	6482	4.9	7281	4.4	9.3
MANIPUR	1420	9.8	1786	11.1	8.8
MEGHALAYA	78	0.9	143	1.4	4.3
MIZORAM	NR		19	0.2	1.1
NAGALAND	84	0.7	110	1.1	1.8
ORISSA	567	1.6	915	2.3	2.1
PUNJAB	0		214	0.3	1.6
RAJASTHAN	2311	3.6	506	0.7	8.5
SIKKIM	3	0.1	3	0.1	1.4
TAMIL NADU	4180	5.2	3135	3.5	5.6
TRIPURA	2000	13.4	924	4.1	8.0
UTTAR PRADESH	6663	4.3	7558	5.5	15.8
UTTARANCHAL	348	2.9	347	2.3	11.9
WEST BENGAL	6099	7.3	6167	7.8	22.4
A & N ISLANDS	265	9.5	242	8.8	8.2
CHANDIGARH	12	0.3	12	0.3	3.9
D & N HAVELI	3	1.3	3	1.4	3.0
DAMAN & DIU	NR		7	3.2	7.8
DELHI	1251	2.2	1229	2.0	11.7
LAKSHADWEEP	3	0.9	2	0.6	95.5
PONDICHERRY	47	2.9	66	2.9	
TOTAL (ALL-INDIA)	103545	8.4	98462	7.0	13.4

Compiled from Crime in India- various annual publications, NCRB (2010)

Chapter 7
Policing Minorities in the Arab World

Nabil Quassini and Arvind Verma

Introduction

Recently many academics, policy makers, practitioners, and activists have become increasingly interested in the study of the relationship between police and minorities around the world (Bowling and Phillips 2002; Chan 1997; Hasisi 2008). The interaction between the police and minorities in the Arab states involves the analysis of the various historical, legal, social, political, and religious characteristics of the nation. Unlike the customary image of being homogeneously Arab and Muslim, the Arab world is home to many indigenous and extraneous majorities and minorities that form a wide range of distributions. Most Arab countries have a majority Muslim population with various religious minorities. A few countries are Muslim with large minorities of non-Arabs and there are others that have minorities that are neither Arab nor Muslim. In each of these circumstances examining the relationship between the police and minorities is essential. The relationship and approaches exercised by each government have implications on how the police view their own minorities and explain the strategies police adopt towards them. Meanwhile, the approaches can also account for the social environment that produces group differences in crime and explicate whether minorities view their experiences with police individually or collectively as members of a particular minority group. In the following chapter, we explore some of these relationships and identify the strategies various Arab governments are using to police their minorities. We focus primarily on case studies from Egypt, Lebanon, and Saudi Arabia to examine the relationship between distinct minorities and the police in these Arab-Muslim dominated societies.

F.B. Hakeem et al., *Policing Muslim Communities: Comparative International Context*,
DOI 10.1007/978-1-4614-3552-5_7, © Springer Science+Business Media New York 2012

Background

Located in North Africa and the Middle East, the Arab world consists of a population of around 350 million people spread across 22 different nations. When combined, the Arab world is larger than some of the world's largest nations, including Brazil, Canada, China, India, and the United States. Each one of these 22 nations considers Arabic as its official language and belongs to an organization called the League of Arab States. The Arab world consists of different forms of governments that vary from monarchies in Morocco, Jordan, and most of the Gulf States to republics or meaningless democracies in the vast majority of the Arab world with either a life-long president or a single political party as was the case in both Tunisia and Egypt. In the past, the Arab world was governed by various forms of caliphates, dynasties, kingdoms, and sultanates that established legal systems that were based on the Islamic religion. These included the Islamic Umayyad and Abbasid dynasties, as well as many other smaller ones spread throughout the Arab world. The most notable was the Turkish Ottoman Empire that virtually ruled the entire Arab world with the exception of Morocco for around four centuries. The Ottomans developed an Islamic legal system known as the millet system (Jaber 1967) for its diverse conquered subjects. The millet system allowed the empire's ethnic and religious minorities to establish their own independent laws and courts as well as manage and regulate their own communities' affairs. It is in the Islamic legal tradition or the sharia and all its derivatives that the historical relationship between religious minorities and the Muslim majority in the Arab world can be examined.

Traditionally Muslims in the Arab world divided the non-Muslim populations into two distinct groups. The first group was called the *mu'ahidin*, otherwise known as the non-Muslim populations who came under a Muslim ruler whose rights were defined by a special treaty or contract. The second called *ahl al-dhimma,* or the protected citizens, consisted of the non-Muslim populations that came under a Muslim ruler after a defeat. Both of these categories historically comprised Christians, Jews, Buddhists, Hindus, and other smaller religious groups (Keller 1994). The people of *dhimma* were granted the same rights as the Muslims as long as they paid a special tax called the *jizya* that was similar to the Muslim payment of the *zakat*. In the legal realm, both the *mu'ahidin* and the *ahl al-dhimma* were accommodated with a pre-modern pluralistic legal system. This approach was manifested in the emergence of religious courts designed to ensure that religious minorities had control of their community and its laws. These included Jewish *Halakha* courts as well as various courts managed by Christians of different denominations (Cohen 1995; Masters 2001).

Ideally non-Muslim minorities were supposed to be treated justly in both criminal and civil matters. Unfortunately this was not always the case in practice and problems did occur in the governing of minorities through the different derivatives of Islamic law. Some historians argue that although non-Muslim minorities in the Arab world were rarely persecuted for their religion, discrimination became quite widespread and institutionalized. According to the historian Bernard Lewis

(1984), non-Muslim minorities were discriminated and symbolically mistreated in many social issues that included the control over what they can build, how they practice their religion in public, their inheritance from and marriages to Muslims, as well as their inferior value in blood money compared to the Muslim citizens. Lewis mentions how churches and synagogues were to never be built higher than mosques, how some leaders imposed dress codes on non-Muslims, and how Muslim men could marry Christian and Jewish women while the contrary was outlawed (Lewis 1984). With the mentioned shortcomings, the treatment of minorities under sharia, however, was still more humane and tolerant than other parts of the world up until the seventeenth century (Allievi and Nielsen 2003; Lewis and Churchill 2009). The general approach Muslims presumed towards religious minorities was that of a group of people who were "separate, unequal and protected" (Barkey 2007: 16).

These categories of non-Muslims in classical Islamic law no longer exist in the Arab world. This change in the legal tradition can be attributed to a few factors that include a shift towards a more progressive approach to Islamic law by certain reformers that include Jamal al-Din al-Afghani, Muhammad Abduh, and Rashid Rida, the eventual growth of Western influences over the centuries, and the transformation of the Arab world from archaic dynasties and empires into modern nation states.

Similar to the legal tradition, the political construction of the modern Arab world has been heavily influenced by European colonization. Many scholars of the Arab world consider the modern borders and political regimes as artificial creations that served the colonial entities that controlled them. These imperial policies accomplished numerous goals for the colonial powers that included internal conflict to divide the populace and the institution of a corrupt subordinate ruling class (Hilal 1976). This strategy was perfected by both the British and the French in their colonies throughout North Africa and the Middle East with the most famous example being the Sykes–Picot Agreement (Fromkin 1989) and its consequences. After independence, most of the regimes continued these colonial policies and centralized their power by disregarding the rule of law while repressing any dissent. Many of these leaders were later supported by either the United States or the Soviet Union as the world was divided into two by the Cold War. In Egypt, Gamal Abdel-Nasser had strong support from the U.S.S.R. because of his anti-imperialist stance against the Western world. But after his death, Anwar Sadat shifted Egypt away from the Soviet Union and formed a new strategic relationship with the United States.

Like Egypt, countries such as Lebanon also had both the United States and the Soviet Union actively work directly and by proxy against one another primarily through Lebanon's various political parties. Meanwhile there were other countries that either completely supported the Soviet Union (republics) or the United States (monarchies). Due to its strong ties with the United States, Saudi Arabia repudiated relations with the Soviet Union and other Communist countries while engaging in a propaganda war with Abdel-Nasser. During these years Arab governments were unrestricted in their persecution of all those who opposed them with the full support of either of the Cold War's superpowers. The staunch support for most of these regimes continued throughout the years and ultimately intensified after the attacks on September 11th as many of these governments continued to suppress all opposition under the pretext of fighting terrorism.

It is within the history of the construction and execution of colonial policies that the issues of minorities and policing in the contemporary Arab world must be placed. Understanding the colonial history of a particular Arab nation can help elucidate certain facts about the relationship between minorities and the criminal justice system. First, with the exception of Saudi Arabia, nearly all Arab countries have a mixture of an Islamic and European legal tradition depending on the influence of their former colonizer. Most countries in the Arab world maintain a court system that preserves Islamic law only in personal and family matters while applying civil law (usually French) in all other matters. Countries such as Algeria also have social-ist influences due to the ideological orientation of the state after independence while forms of tribal customary law are still the norm in parts of Jordan, Iraq, and Yemen among others in dealing with the mediation of disputes between Bedouins in those regions.

Second, studying the colonial policies towards minorities in Arab countries reveals how previous colonial powers and current regimes either exploited existing tensions or instigated new ones between various groups for their own purposes. Contrary to the popular oversimplified depiction of the Arab world as homoge-neous, countries in the region vary extensively in their heterogeneity. The Arab world consists of a number of religious, ethnic, and linguistic minorities. There are Jews, Christians of various denominations, and many non-Sunni branches of Islam. Recently in the Arab world there have also been a growing number of Baha'i, Buddhist, and Hindu migrant workers in the Gulf. Many ethnic and linguistic groups include the Armenians, Assyrians, Berbers, Kurds, Turks, as well as other smaller groups. The three nations discussed in this chapter have a significant amount of minorities. Although 99.6% of all Egyptians are categorized as ethnically Egyptian (Central Intelligence Agency 2011), there is a rather large Christian minority that is estimated to be around 12 million people or 15% of the Egyptian population (Minority Rights Group International [MRGI] 2010). As the Arab world's most religiously diverse country, Lebanon has 18 officially recognized sects. The largest of these sects consist of Shiite (28%) and Sunni Muslims (28%), various Christian sects that include the Maronites (21.5%), Greek Orthodox (8%), Greek Catholic (4%), Armenian, Assyrian, Chaldean, Melkite, Protestant, and Syriac churches as well as a sizable amount of Druze (5%) and other smaller populations of Baha'is, Buddhists, Hindus, and Jews (MRGI 2010). Palestinian refugees constitute Lebanon's largest ethnic minority with over 300,000 living in 12 refugee camps spread around the country. According to the U.S. State Department (2009), Saudi Arabia's population of 27 million consists of about 8–10 million foreign nationals from all over the world. Saudi citizens predominantly comprise Sunni Muslims with a Shiite minority of approximately 10–15% that live primarily in the Eastern Province (U.S. State Department 2009).

Similar to the divide-and-conquer techniques employed in other parts of the world, colonial administrators relied on the local power structure to govern these diverse groups. These policies worked well with some groups in the Arab world as their co-operation with colonial powers brought them tremendous power within their communities. There are many examples of these policies, as was the case with the British and their use of Abdel-Aziz Ibn Saud, the first monarch of modern Saudi Arabia to fight and weaken the Ottoman Empire and the House of Rashid. This strategy was particularly useful in sectarian conflicts as certain groups used it to maintain power while others used these opportunities to create a new power structure. The current confessional system in Lebanon that divided institutional power among various religious groups was formulated to ensure that certain Christian groups allied with the French sustained their political dominance. This colonial strategy was embraced by most post-colonial Arab governments as a fundamental part of their authoritarian policies. Through the special use of religion, regimes justify and maintain their political power over the masses while demonizing any group that challenges their legitimacy. The political use of religion by rulers has been a tradition in the pre-modern Muslim world that continues today. The fact that titles such as the "Commander of the Faithful" by the King of Morocco, "The Custodian of the Two Holy Mosques" by the King of Saudi Arabia, or "The Hashemite King" by the King of Jordan are still relevant today confirms the important use of religion in monarchies. These titles still carry important symbolic meaning, as any disloyalty can be construed as a form of treason or even apostasy. By combining successful strategies on the use of religion from both the pre-modern and colonial era, Arab governments have controlled dissent and rebellion aimed at their regimes. As a result, many religious minorities who obviously do not adhere to these religious beliefs are viewed as a threat to the ruler's sacred narrative.

Finally, the colonial policies can help us understand the evolution and development of a country's modern police force. Although most conventional narratives portray the colonial administration's police forces as the apparatus for security and crime control, in reality they were used to protect the imperial economic, social, and political order. The generally militaristic characteristics of policing ensured exploitation while deterring any resistance to the colonial system. This structure of policing is still prevalent around the Arab world. Today, the police remain the most essential institution that safeguards the status quo in Arab countries. It is the police that continue to control today's minorities as well as any other groups within the state that are deemed a threat to the social order and national unity. As the rest of the world progressed, patterns of policing in the Arab world remained untouched as most states continued to use the highly centralized colonial Irish model of policing. Public confidence in the criminal justice system remains quite low in the Arab world as the use of political authoritarianism is the norm.

The relationship between police and minorities has also been problematic. Minorities continue to grow cynical as they perceive the police forces as unjust, corrupt, and quite often incompetent. Case studies of Egypt, Lebanon, and Saudi Arabia will be presented to examine how minorities are handled by the criminal justice system and police in these particular Muslim-dominated societies. Egypt's Copts represent the largest Christian minority in the Arab world and have been underrepresented and mistreated by Egypt's police forces since the era of British occupation. Lebanon's confessional political system has divided its political and religious communities, yet all confessions are in agreement against the idea of *tawteen* or the permanent settling of Palestinians in Lebanon. As Lebanon's largest minority, Palestinian refugees have lived for years independently in camps as "states within a state." The recent conflict in the Nahr el-Bared refugee camp has created an experimental security model that gives the Lebanese government the opportunity to rearrange completely the policing and security of Palestinian refugee camps. The historical alliance between the al-Saud family and the religious leader Mohamed ibn Abdel-Wahab in the eighteenth century established the Saudi monarchy and has institutionalized a puritanical form of Sunni Islam as the official doctrine of the state. The union has often placed the monarchy and its security forces at odds with its minorities that include the indigenous Shiite population and the millions of migrant workers of different nationalities, ethnic groups, and religions that make a living in Saudi Arabia.

Egypt

During the nineteenth century reign of Muhammad Ali, the Egyptian police were heavily influenced by indigenous, Ottoman, and French systems of policing. However, Egypt's modern police force was established during the British occupation that occurred after Muhammad Ali's death. In the early years of occupation, the British preserved the policing system that they found in Egypt. Despite the Egyptians' resistance and deep resentment towards the occupation and its policies, the British colonial administration managed ultimately to take control and change the policing system through an arduous political struggle against the Egyptian government (Tolefson 1999). Similar to the British colonization of Ireland and India, the British colonial police in Egypt developed a military model of policing that protected the status quo and suppressed any uprisings against the British colonial administration. The Egyptian colonial police excelled in the use of heavy-handed tactics towards any upheaval but had difficulty in responding to common everyday crime. Even after Egypt's independence, the Egyptian monarchy eventually controlled most government institutions and adopted many of the control strategies used by the British. The police force remained highly centralized and worked primarily for the monarchy.

Gamal Abdel Nasser's coup d'état against the monarchy in 1952 transformed the new republic into a police state that created an abhorrence for the police by the general population. After Nasser's death, Anwar Sadat introduced new reforms and policies in a strategy to modernize the security apparatus as he politically shifted Egypt away from the Soviet Union and more towards the United States. During his presidency the Police Authority Law was passed establishing the president as the chief of the police while the minister of interior became known as the superior of police with direct control over every governor and director of police spread throughout Egypt's provinces. The law also made sure that a file was kept for every police officer with reports on the quality of his work (Onwudiwe 2006). The reforms introduced were insufficient and the policing system remained the same nevertheless. Sadat's assassination in 1981 gave the new president Hosni Mubarak wider powers through the re-emergence of Egypt's emergency laws. These laws permitted the president to sidestep the constitution by extending police powers, and suspending various constitutional rights. Reminiscent of the Nasser years, Mubarak restricted all political opposition and responded ruthlessly to any dissent. The declaration of war by radical Islamic groups in the early 1990s put an end to any discussion by reformists on repealing the emergency laws as the Mubarak regime gained international support for its uncompromising iron-fisted approach to counterterrorism. In the subsequent years, the Mubarak regime promised numerous times to repeal the emergency laws but continued to extend them although it had been decades since Sadat's assassination and the threat of terrorism by radical Islamists had subsided.

The British have had a long-lasting influence on Egypt's policing system that continued to function the same way to a certain extent until the fall of Mubarak. While the British structured the police in the customary military fashion, subsequent Egyptian regimes sustained a similar centralized hierarchy directly controlled by the interior minister and the president to ensure the police force's absolute loyalty. There have been numerous grievances against the police forces throughout the years that have become famous memorable slogans used against the Mubarak regime in Cairo's Tahrir Square. These grievances include the use of the state's emergency laws by security forces to detain and imprison anyone for an indefinite amount of time, police torture, brutality, and corruption. Throughout Egypt's modern history the police forces have neglected their roles of protecting and serving the public and enforced the law primarily when it was in the regime's interests. Along with the traditional functions of policing, the Egyptian national police force worked to silence any dissent and safeguard the regime. These strategies were revealed to the world in the numerous incidents during the revolution against Mubarak including the memorable deployment of plain-clothed police officers riding camels and horses to suppress protestors.

Egypt's Copts

Coptic Christians represent the largest minority in Egypt with roughly 10–15% of the population. Around 90% of Copts belong to the Coptic Orthodox Church of Alexandria making it one of the largest and oldest Christian communities in the Arab world. Historically, relations between the Muslim majority and the Coptic minority have been uneasy with certain periods of stability and tolerance as well as other times of hardship and persecution. The modern relationship between the Egyptian security apparatus and its largest religious minority began in the reign of Muhammad Ali Pasha in the early nineteenth century. During this period of time, the relationship between Copts and Muslims progressed through Muhammad Ali's transformation of Egypt into a regional power. However, after Muhammad Ali's death, Egypt's encounter with British occupation entrenched the colonial policies towards the Copts that continue to endure.

Along with rearranging the police, the British also created policies that turned the majority Muslim population against the Copts. The British commissioner, for example, established a system of excluding Copts from any high positions in the government (Kyriakos 1911). The Copts reacted through a congress in Asyut that discussed several grievances that included the exemption of working on religious holidays, equal access to administrative posts, government grants, and representatives in the provincial councils (Meinardus 2002). During Egypt's struggle for independence, the relationship between Copts and Muslims improved as they united with the revolutionary Sa'ad Zaghlul, in their fight against the British occupation and creation of a new independent state. Copts in particular enjoyed their status with their peers as a result of their contributions to Egyptian sovereignty and independence. Unfortunately for all Egyptians, the monarchy adopted many of the strategies used by the British against the Copts.

Gamal Abdel Nasser's relationship with the Copts was complex. As a socialist, Nasser was an ardent secularist that clamped down on both radical and moderate Islamists, a move welcomed by many Copts though it was used primarily to consolidate power. At the same time, Nasser's program of nationalizing various private enterprises affected many prominent and affluent Coptic families. Most Copts believe that Nasser's regime failed to address the grievances declared in Asyut around 50 years earlier that continued to exist, including the exclusion of Copts from important government positions. When Anwar Sadat succeeded Nasser after his death in 1970, Copts felt worse as Sadat enacted policies that favored Islamists. In reality, Sadat used the Islamists as a strategy to counter left-wing radicals that threatened his power. Many Copts were also troubled with the Egyptian government's intrusion into the Coptic Church that included Sadat's internal exile of the Pope Shenouda III who was eventually reinstated by Mubarak in 1985.

During Mubarak's 30-year regime, the Coptic community felt even more vulnerable as they became the target of many hate crimes and terrorist attacks. Although there were mob attacks on Copts throughout the 1970s and 1980s, the declaration of war against the government in the early 1990s by radical Islamic groups had a greater impact on the Copts as they became the focus of numerous terrorist attacks targeting Coptic businesses, houses, and places of worship. In the beginning of the millennium, interreligious riots gained widespread attention in the southern city of al-Kosheh as 20 Copts were killed. Recent events include the Nag Hammadi massacre in 2010 that resulted in the deaths of nine Copts as they walked out of a cathedral on the Coptic Christmas eve. In May of 2010 there were mob attacks against the Coptic community in Marsa Matrouh as well as the 2011 New Year's Eve car bomb that killed 21 people in front of the Alexandria's Coptic Orthodox Church that made international headlines.

Despite Mubarak's persistence that he was the best leader to protect the Coptic community and keep it safe, the relationship between the Copts and the police throughout the years of Mubarak's Egypt was strained due to the government's passive response to these incidents. In each of the cases mentioned above the Egyptian police were incompetent in the prevention and investigations of the attacks on the Copts. In most cases the police were even accused of being complicit in the crimes by either arriving late after all the violence was over or by simply favoring the attackers over the victims. This strategy became the norm during the Mubarak regime as a means of fostering division amongst Egyptians. This allegation is facilitated in view of the fact that the policy of excluding Copts from many important positions in the government has changed little since British colonialism. Copts continue to be underrepresented in many institutions in Egypt that include law enforcement and state security. Many Coptic activists contend that the Mubarak regime condones the violence against them and has completely disregarded the right of their community's security and safety guaranteed in the constitution.

After the January 25th revolution, both Copts and Muslims are feeling uncertain about their future under the new rulers of Egypt, the Supreme Council of the Armed Forces (SCAF). Despite Mubarak's resignation and the dissolution of his National Democratic Party (NDP), Egyptians remain apprehensive of SCAF's monopoly of power and continue to increase protests demanding that SCAF transfer authority to civilians. The news coming out of Egypt indicates that these fears are warranted. The curtailing of the media, protests, and other freedoms of expression along with the military trials of civilians, continued violations of human rights, and the delay in the prosecution of Mubarak, his sons, and other former senior officials from the NDP reveals that SCAF is preserving its acquired position and privileges the same way Mubarak preserved the status quo during his tenure as president. SCAF is also demanding a troubling new role in the future of Egypt in the discussion on drafting a constitution as it insists on adding supraconstitutional provisions that would allow it purportedly to protect the constitution's legitimacy.

The current situation in Egypt is unpredictable for the Coptic community. Many Copts are pessimistic about Egypt's future in light of the carnage that occurred near the Maspero building in Cairo. Copts joined by some Muslims protesting against Field Marshal Mohamed Tantawi and the governor of the Aswan province Mustafa Kamal al-Sayyed were assaulted by security forces using live ammunition, tear gas, and armored personnel carriers resulting in 27 deaths and over 212 injuries. Egyptian state media controlled by SCAF reported the incident in flagrantly sectarian terms and refused any responsibility on the part of the armed forces for the deaths and violence (Human Rights Watch [HRW] 2011a). Protests by both Copts and Muslims continue to call for an investigation of the violence. Only with the transfer of power from the SCAF to civilians and a future democratic state that is accountable to all its citizens regardless of religion can the prospects appear positive for all Egyptians.

Lebanon

Lebanon's modern police force was established in 1861 with the Lebanese Gendarmerie (Internal Security Forces 2005). As part of the Ottoman Empire, Lebanon was later occupied by the French after the Ottomans sided with the Austrians and Germans during World War I. The French inherited the Arab world's most religiously diverse country in one of the most strategic locations in the Middle

East. The French enforced a system of government that distributed political power proportional to Lebanon's religious communities as a means of controlling the new mandated territory. The new confessional system became the norm as it guaranteed the political dominance of France's Maronite allies and required the president to be a Maronite Christian, the prime minister a Sunni Muslim, and the speaker of the parliament a Shiite Muslim. The new system also required that the seats in parliament be divided between Christians and Muslims by a 6:5 ratio. The president's veto power over any legislation ensured that the ratio never changed even when the population's distribution did. The confessional system eventually spread through most public institutions that included the universities, the media, the military, and the police MRGI (2011a).

From the time of its independence the police and gendarmerie worked separately until both were integrated in 1959 to form the Internal Security Force (ISF) under the ministry of the interior. The ISF and all its various branches including the judiciary police, territorial gendarmerie, and the criminal investigations division among others, still are accountable to the ministry of the interior and fall under all of its regulations and directives. The ISF is composed of a fixed ratio of Lebanon's various religious groups that tended to work primarily in the vicinities that included members of their own religion. The Lebanese Armed Forces (LAF) also played a supportive role to the ISF and at times arbitrated between the various political parties. Unfortunately, during the Lebanese Civil War from 1975 to 1990, the LAF became a supporter of the Maronite Christian president and both the ISF and LAF became weak as members from all religious persuasions defected to sectarian militias with the help and finance of different foreign nations. After 15 years of civil war, the Lebanese government finally reached a new agreement that addressed some of the disparities between confessions that led to a more balanced representation of both Christians and Muslims that is reflected in today's Lebanese police forces.

Although the ISF and LAF consist of a multisectarian force, both continue to be constrained by the Lebanese confessional political system even after the 1989 Taif Agreement (Norton 1991). Other than balancing the representation of religions, the confessional system still exists in most Lebanese institutions. Recruitment into the police for example, continues to be regulated with an obligation to confessional diversity. However, due to the weakness of Lebanon's political confessional system many external forces continue to influence Lebanese foreign and domestic affairs. The greatest security challenges that both the ISF and LAF face involves the persistent support and intervention sought by Lebanese politicians of various religious sects and political groups from foreign countries. The interference and influences of foreign states on Lebanon's affairs continues only to divide and impair the Lebanese. In recent years, the assassination of Rafik Hariri, the 2006 conflict between Hezbollah and Israel, the Doha Agreement, and the Nahr al-Bared conflict are only a few examples of how the division that exists in Lebanon can escalate to violence and complicate the Lebanese police forces' work. Many Lebanese are calling for the replacement of the confessional system for a more merit-based approach (Mouassaoui 2011). Rather than focusing on equal religious representation the government should focus on educating the new generations on the virtues of understanding through tolerance.

Palestinians in Lebanon

Many Lebanese believe that the historical tensions and political conflicts between confessions were amplified by the arrival of Palestinian refugees who started migrating in 1948 and 1967 from Israel and today constitute Lebanon's largest minority group. More than 300,000 Palestinians live in 12 refugee camps spread throughout Lebanon. In the first few decades, Palestinian refugees were policed by the LAF's internal security services, the Second Bureau or the *Deuxième Bureau*. Resembling the model of policing in the region, the *Deuxième Bureau* had a reputation of harsh heavy-handed tactics that rigidly controlled the Palestinians. The policing of the refugee camps, however, changed when Egypt's Abdel-Nasser helped negotiate the Cairo Agreement in 1969 between the LAF and the Palestinian Liberation Organization (PLO). The LAF agreed to withdraw from all Palestinian refugee camps and allocated all security responsibilities to the PLO. The agreement occurred within the years the PLO and thousands of Palestinian fighters were expelled from Jordan after the events of Black September. Many Lebanese political and religious groups were wary of the agreement, as the assembly of Palestinian resistance groups and the increase of activities was seen as a threat to Lebanese sovereignty and the country's delicate confessional demographics. Due to these and many other factors, civil war broke out in 1975 and security forces disintegrated into militias of different ideological, nationalist, and religious groups. During the civil war, both Israel and Syria occupied different parts of Lebanon while multinational forces ensured that the PLO was expelled. In the aftermath, the Lebanese government withdrew from the Cairo Agreement and restored their jurisdiction over all Palestinian refugee camps yet refrained from entering any of them. Instead of directly controlling the camps, the Lebanese government authorized a new arrangement inside the camps in the establishment of popular committees to rule the camps politically and security committees to function as the internal police force.

The security arrangement between the Lebanese government and the popular and security committees continue to function in most camps in a coherent manner. The popular committees represent the refugee camps and deal with issues related to culture, education, health, and other essential economic and social services. The network of security committee members, UNRWA camp officers, and members of different Palestinian political factions police the camps and co-operate with the ISF whenever needed. Unfortunately the Nahr el-Bared conflict in 2007 was the catalyst to a new security model that will replace the popular and security committees with both the ISF and LAF.

The conflict started in the Nahr el-Bared refugee camp (NBC) when an armed Islamic extremist group called Fatah al-Islam overran the camp after skirmishes with the camp's residents and security committees (Abboud 2009). Fatah al-Islam easily established themselves in the NBC due to several reasons that include inadequate training of the security committees, the lack of control of arms into the camps, the weakness of the Palestinian leadership, and the Lebanese government's refusal to intercede (Rougier 2008). The Lebanese government was finally forced to confront the extremist group after 13 LAF soldiers were killed at a military check-point by Fatah al-Islam militants. For the next 15 weeks the LAF battled Fatah al-Islam members in the NBC with more than 50 civilians, 179 LAF soldiers, and 226 members of Fatah al-Islam killed in the conflict. The indiscriminate bombing reduced the NBC to rubble and left over $300,000 million worth of damage as well as over 33,000 refugees fleeing from the violence (United Nations Relief and Works Agency 2008).

In the destruction of the NBC, the Lebanese government is implementing a community policing program to directly administer the NBC's security using the ISF. The program will serve as an experimental security model planned for all other Palestinian refugee camps in Lebanon. To prevent future armed extremist groups from taking over any of Lebanon's refugee camps, the United States has spent $100 million in training and equipping the ISF since 2007, including community policing programs sponsored by the U.S. Department of State (Addis 2011). However, many Palestinians are skeptical of the community policing program discussed by the Lebanese government. Palestinians believe that the campaign carried out by the LAF against Fatah al-Islam members hiding in the NBC was excessive and preventable if they had trusted and included members of the security committee in the operations. Palestinian refugees believe the indiscriminate bombing of the camp was unnecessary and that they were victimized by the LAF's destruction of a refugee camp that they have built for 60 years. Along with the LAF's approach to fighting Fatah al-Islam, Palestinian refugees are suspicious of the LAF's unilateral approach to security. The ISF and LAF's policing of the NBC does not have any community oversight and security forces remain unaccountable to anyone among the NBC refugees. Mutually, the Lebanese mistrust the Palestinians due to their perception of how Palestinians historically intensified tensions between confessions, caused the 15-year civil war and occupations by both the Israelis and the Syrians. Furthermore, one of the few political issues that all confessions agree to oppose is *tawteen* or the permanent settling of Palestinian refugees in Lebanon. If it remains unaddressed, the lack of trust between the two will destabilize any policing policies made by the Lebanese government towards Palestinian refugee camps.

The current policing experiment in the NBC by the Lebanese has been a failure so far (Palestinian Human Rights Organization 2011; HRW 2011b). Most Palestinians reject the policing of their refugee camps by Lebanese security forces. Even worse than the unilateral approach by the Lebanese government to security is the discrimination faced by Palestinian refugees in their status as an unwelcome foreign minority despite the fact that they have lived in Lebanon for three generations. In Lebanon, Palestinian refugees still have no right to an education, work, housing, or healthcare (HRW 2011b). Lebanese politicians continue to justify their denial of basic human rights for Palestinians using the fear of *tawteen* or their permanent settlement in Lebanon. Any plans for police forces to work with Palestinian refugees must address Palestinian rights and include the discrimination, inequality, and poverty faced in their day-to-day lives without negating the Palestinians' right to negotiate their future plans for a state.

Saudi Arabia

Historically the diverse tribes in Arabia lived in separate territories and competed for supremacy over the Arabian peninsula. Throughout the past couple of centuries the Khalidis, Hashimis, and Rashidis all controlled large portions of the peninsula at one time or another. The Ottomans also ruled parts of the Arabian peninsula with the co-operation of these tribes. The story behind the current Saudi monarchy starts in the eighteenth century when an alliance was made between the Saud family and the religious leader Mohamed Ibn Abdel-Wahab. The intermarriage between the Saudis and Ibn Abdel-Wahab's religious ideology helped the Saudis establish themselves as one of the most powerful tribes in Arabia. The religious ideology is regularly referred to as the "Wahabi" sect, though most Saudis find the term offensive and describe themselves as the followers of the early generations of Muslims (U.S. Department of State 2010). With the use of Ibn Abdel-Wahab's ideology, the Saudi tribe legitimized their claim to power by religiously differentiating themselves from other tribes. After two unsuccessful attempts to create a state, the Saudis finally established a monarchy under Abdel-Aziz ibn Saud with the help of a group of Bedouin religious fundamentalists called the Ikhwan against other tribes in Arabia, and with the help of the British against the Ottomans. The Ikhwan later rebelled against King Abdel-Aziz when he refused to let them expand in neighboring British protectorates. With further assistance from the British, King Abdel-Aziz defeated the Ikhwan's rebellion in the Battle of Sabilla and reorganized them into the Saudi Arabian National Guard.

King Abdel-Aziz acquired the same security structure that the Ottoman Empire had used for the previous centuries. Policing during this period was informal and crime was investigated by tribal leaders while the Ottomans provided support when needed. In the first years of the monarchy, the Saudi Arabian National Guard took on a similar role in policing the tribes and preventing rebellion or intertribal conflict. Saudi Arabia's modern police were established with the formation of the ministry of the interior and divided the responsibilities of policing into three groups that include the regular police, the secret police, and the religious police (Dammer et al. 2006) that were also assisted by the military when needed. The regular police or the Public Security Forces (PSF) recruit members from all regions of the countries and from different tribes so that they can maintain law and order at the local, provincial, and national levels. The units in the PSF fall under the control of a provincial governor and the director of public safety. The secret police or the *mubahith* gather intelligence and work directly for the minister of the interior. Both police forces remain centralized with a hierarchical line of command that leads directly to the king (Varghese 2010). The religious police officially called the Committee to Prevent Vice and Promote Virtue or the *mutawwa'un* in Arabic enforce the Saudi interpretation of social Islamic norms. Part of their duties includes the prevention of women from driving cars, intermingling between men and women in public, un-Islamic acts that range from sorcery or magic, to acts of lewdness that could lead to illicit sexual relations (Dammer et al. 2006). The *mutawwa'un,* report to the king through the council of ministers and though the minister of the interior coordinates with the *mutawaa'un*, it does not have any authority over them (U.S. State Department 2009). According to the International Religious Freedom Report (2010), there are more than 5,000 staff members in all 13 provinces and the *mutawwa'un* were not allowed to work officially unless they were accompanied by a police officer. The *mutawwa'un* have been in conflict with many of Saudi Arabia's minorities and have earned a reputation for their intolerance.

Saudi Shiites

Saudi Arabia's largest indigenous minority are the Shiites who live primarily in the Eastern and Najran Provinces and in the city of Medina. Shiites are about 10–15% of the total Saudi native population (U.S. State Department 2009). Since establishing the monarchy, the Saudi kingdom's ultraconservative interpretation of Sunni Islam has permitted "zealots [to] implement … a repressive religious policy" (Louer 2008: 21). The relationship between the Saudi monarchy and the Shiites degenerated after Khomeini's revolution in Iran. During those days, many Saudi Shiites took to the streets to celebrate Khomeini's return and the holiday of *Ashura*, while others organized demonstrations and went on strikes (al-Rasheed 1998). The Saudi police forces brutally repressed these public displays of faith by the Shiites and decided to counter the influence from the Iranian Revolution by investing and improving the infrastructure of the predominately Shiite regions. These events increased support for the propagation of the Saudi government's interpretation of Islam and escalated institutional discrimination on the Shiite minority who was now seen as a fifth column working with the new Iranian regime. Currently the monarchy limits political participation in the government to a handful of Shiites with the expectation that they would manage any dissent rising from their communities (Nasr 2006).

In the realm of criminal justice, the Shiites are habitually abused by the police forces and their testimonies in court are given less credence than those of other Sunni Saudis (MRGI 2011b). According to Human Rights Watch (2009), police forces prohibit Shiites from publicly celebrating special holidays, arrested them during the pilgrimage for practicing their interpretations of Islamic rituals, organizing their own Quranic studies, and for selling special clothes for religious ceremonies. Discrimination occurs in religious matters, education, justice, and the workforce through the exclusion of Shiites from certain jobs (HRW 2009). Shiites are underrepresented in many of the significant positions in the police and military and were more likely to work in subordinate positions as traffic and lower-level officers in Shiite municipalities (U.S. State Department 2009).

The protests in the past year in the Arab world have also inspired the Shiites of Saudi Arabia. The Bahraini government's reaction to the neighboring Pearl Revolution has angered the local Shiite population and many of the communities' grievances remerged. The protests in Bahrain that called for equality between the Shiite majority and the Sunni monarchy were viciously quelled when Saudi tanks and troops rode into Bahrain. The Shiite community in Saudi Arabia has shown solidarity with the Bahraini Shiites and started their own demands for equality, respect for their religious identity, and the release of their community's political prisoners. Recently the protests have escalated as police forces have opened fire and killed a handful of protestors in the past few months.

Saudi Migrant Workers

Saudi Arabia's largest minority population consists of around 8 million legal migrant workers and an estimated population of 10 million when including the undocumented migrant workers (HRW 2011c; U.S. State Department 2009). The approximate nationalities of workers provided by embassies in Riyadh reveal that 1.8 million workers are Indians, 1.5 million Bangladeshis, 1.4 million Filipinos, 1 million Egyptians, as well as thousands of other migrant workers of various nationalities (U.S. State Department 2009). Demographics on religious denominations are not obtainable but based on their nationalities the migrant workers come from a diverse amount of religious backgrounds that include various types of Muslims, Christians, Jews, Hindus, Buddhists, Sikhs, and other religious groups. The Saudi ministry of economy and planning asserts that foreigners maintain 67% of the country's labor force (Center for Democracy and Human Rights in Saudi Arabia [CDHR] 2011). Although the Saudi economy would disintegrate without these workers, according to Human Rights Watch (2011c) many of them are regularly exploited and abused. The report described how workers cannot change jobs or leave the country once they are in Saudi Arabia unless they have written consent from their sponsors while others were simply held as hostages when they have had their passports confiscated. Other workers described various forms of severe physical, verbal, psychological, and sexual abuse from their employers (HRW 2011c). In Saudi Arabia there are no agencies that can address any grievances and migrant workers do not have access to the justice system (CDHR 2011). Police forces usually side with the Saudi employers and are known to turn away from complaints made by migrant workers. The level of discrimination in Saudi Arabia is excessive to the point that African and Asian workers are paid less than their American and European co-workers for performing the exact same jobs (Atiyyah 1996; Kanovsky 1986).

Along with facing abuse and discrimination, the experiences of migrant workers are made even worse when their religious and social rights are taken into account. Any public form of worship outside of Islam is forbidden and the *mutawwa'un* along with security forces of the ministry of the interior continuously raid private non-Islamic religious gatherings and confiscate non-Islamic religious material (U.S. State Department 2009). Many foreigners have become the targets of harassment by the *mutawwa'un* for failure to observe a modest dress code or because they intermingled with members of the opposite sex. Currently, there are no non-Muslim houses of worship in all of Saudi Arabia; Muslims can still be executed for converting to other sects or religions, while any proselytizing by non-Muslims remains illegal (U.S. State Department 2009). Many migrant workers continue to comply with the rules out of fear of losing their jobs and being deported. There are also media reports that describe the *mutawwa'un*'s duties of detecting and arresting practitioners of witchcraft and black magic. Many of those arrested are from parts of the world that engage in traditional healing practices (U.S. State Department 2009).

The Saudi government has in the past few years attempted to improve both its image and its relationship with minorities in several ways. The government has worked on training the *mutawaa'un* to improve their performance and decrease their harassment of religious minorities. There were occasions when the Saudi government stepped in and disciplined the *mutawwa'un* for certain complaints raised by foreigners. The media has even recently covered the trials of certain members of the *mutawwa'un* who had overstepped their duties (U.S. State Department 2009). Human rights officials are now starting to have a greater amount of capacity to work in certain segments of society to which they did not have access. In recent years there have been fewer reports of Saudi officials confiscating religious materials. To address the Shiite community, in 2004 King Abdullah started the National Dialogue sessions with Shiite religious leaders that included discussions on the release of political prisoners and a more balanced representation of Shiites in the government (U.S. State Department 2009). The Saudi legal system has also worked to include different interpretations of Islamic law and has continued to permit Shiites to use their own legal tradition when adjudicating noncriminal cases. The King has also created the Interfaith Dialogue Initiative to promote tolerance and religious moderation among various countries from around the world. Though these steps were welcomed by the international community, many question this initiative and argue that the measure of tolerance should be what is practiced in the kingdom rather than what is discussed overseas.

Conclusion

The three Arab countries discussed in this chapter are examples of the Arab world's complex heterogeneity. Egypt is a country with a significant Arab non-Muslim minority; Palestinians continue to struggle in refugee camps in the Arab world's most religiously diverse country; while Shiites and foreigners continue to struggle in Saudi Arabia due to their religious beliefs. In the analysis of each country, police interaction with the minorities depended primarily on the state's position on those minorities. In Egypt, the police interaction between Copts depended on the regime's perception of how the minority can be controlled and exploited. During British occupation, the Copts were treated unjustly to keep the Muslim majority from revolting against occupation. In some regimes the Copts were controlled and used to divide Egyptian society in religious sectarian terms, while others safeguarded their positions by posing as their only neutral protector. The interaction between Lebanon's police and Palestinian refugees had always been minimal. The recent conflict in Nahr el-Bared is changing the relationship between the two peoples. Lebanese politicians of various religious and political confessions continue to use the concept of *tawteen* to demonstrate Lebanese nationalism while instilling unnecessary fear of Palestinian refugees living in Lebanon. Palestinian refugees are continuously used by the Lebanese as a scapegoat for all the problems Lebanon has experienced in the past few decades and thus far the policing of the Nahr el-Bared refugee camp reflects those attitudes. The Saudi monarchy has also used its Shiite minority to create cohesion among the followers of the state's interpretation of Islam while protecting itself from Iranian influence in its predominately Shiite regions. The Saudi exploitation of their migrant workers reflects its perception of that community as external and inequitable to other Saudis. The interaction between police with both the Shiite community and migrant workers reflects the government's religious intolerance and its own zealous devotion to the teachings of Ibn Abdel-Wahab.

This is unfortunate for the Arab world, and particularly these countries have the resources to address inequalities and construct an equitable society. These nations, particularly Saudi Arabia, exert a considerable amount of influence on the Muslims of the world because of their association with the establishment of Islam in this region. All the major Islamic holy sites are located here and what happens in these countries is closely followed across the world. If these nations could set an example of treating their minorities humanely and give equal rights this would set an example for the rest of the world and mitigate the animosity against the Muslim community. At present, the discrimination and venomous environment against the Muslim minorities is reinforced by the perception that Muslim majorities do not treat their own minorities properly. The demand to establish mosques, wear the hijab, and propagate their religion in democratic societies is questioned by other communities who find that these Muslim majority nations deny them such rights in their regions. Right-wing groups in India, the Netherlands, and the United Kingdom have opposed demands by the Muslims to follow their religion when the Muslims do not reciprocate similarly where they dominate.

Furthermore, democratic ideals are based on the concept of equality, acceptance of diversity and freedom of belief. These are largely guaranteed in western democracies and in mixed societies such as India and Israel. The denial of these ideals to different minorities in Muslim majority regions suggests that Islamic jurisprudence does not permit these concepts. This is obviously wrong for Islam preaches equality and nondiscrimination. But practices and police functions in Muslim majority nations suggest otherwise and reinforce the perception that Islam mistreats followers of other religions. It is imperative that these nations, particularly Saudi Arabia, implement policies that are truly based on the faith that stands for peace and harmony.

References

Abboud, S. (2009). The Siege of Nahr al-Bared and the Palestinian Refugees in Lebanon. *Arab Studies Quarterly, 31*, 31–48.

Addis, C. L. (2011). *U.S. Security Assistance to Lebanon*. CRS report for congress, congressional research service, 19 Jan 2011. Retrieved from http://knxasl.hsdl.org/?view&doc=137765&coll =limited.

Allievi, S., & Nielsen, J. (Eds.). (2003). *Muslim networks and transnational communities in and across Europe*. Leiden: Brill.

Al-Rasheed, M. (1998). The Shia of Saudi Arabia: A minority in search of cultural authenticity. *British Journal of Middle Eastern Studies, 25*(1), 121–138.

Atiyyah, H. S. (1996). Expatriates acculturation in Arab Gulf countries. *Journal of Management Development, 15*(5), 37–47.

Barkey, K. (2007). Islam and toleration: Studying the Ottoman imperial model. *International Journal of Politics, Culture and Society, 19*(1–2), 5–19.

Bowling, B., & Phillips, C. (2002). *Racism, crime and justice*. Harlow: Longman.

Center for Democracy and Human Rights in Saudi Arabia. (2011). *Minority rights*. Retrieved from http://www.cdhr.info/index.php?option=com_content&view=category&layout=bog&id=39&Itemid=70.

Central Intelligence Agency. (2011). *Egypt*. Retrieved from www.cia.gov/library/publications/the-world-factbook/geos/eg.html.

Chan, J. (1997). *Changing police culture: Policing in a multicultural society*. Cambridge: Cambridge University Press.

Cohen, M. R. (1995). *Under crescent and cross: The Jews in the middle ages*. Princeton: Princeton University Press.

Dammer, H. R., Fairchild, E., & Albanese, J. S. (2006). *Comparative criminal justice systems* (3rd ed.). Blemont: Wadsworth/Thomas.

Fromkin, D. (1989). *A peace to end all peace: The fall of the Ottoman Empire and the creation of the Modern Middle East*. New York: H. Holt.

Hasisi, B. (2008) Police, politics, and culture in a deeply divided society. *The Journal of Criminal Law & Criminology, 98*, 1119–1146.

Hilal, A. E. (1976). A-tajzi'a wat-taqsim fi al-watan al-'arabi (Division and Fragmentation in the Arab Homeland), *Qadaia 'arabiyya* (Beirut) 3, nos. 1–6. http://www.palhumanrights.org/rep/ENG/Camp%20in%20FearCamp%20in%20Want_Final-A4.pdf.

Human Rights Watch. (2009). *Saudi Arabia treat Shia equally*. New York: Human Rights Watch, Inc. Retrieved from http://www.hrw.org/news/2009/09/02/saudi-arabia-treat-shia-equally.

Human Rights Watch. (2011). *Egypt: Don't cover up military killing of Copt protesters*. New York: Human Rights Watch, Inc. Retrieved from http://www.hrw.org/news/2011/10/25/egypt-don-t-cover-military-killing-copt-protesters.

Human Rights Watch. (2011). *World report 2011: Lebanon*. New York: Human Rights Watch, Inc. Retrieved from http://www.hrw.org/world-report-2011/lebanon.

Human Rights Watch. (2011). *World report 2011: Saudi Arabia*. New York: Human Rights Watch, Inc. Retrieved from http://www.hrw.org/world-report-2011/saudiarabia.

Internal Security Forces. (2005). Historical Overview. http://www.isf.gov.lb/English/LeftMenu/General%20Info/History/Pages/History.spx. Accessed 2 Nov 2011.

Jaber, K. S. A. (1967). The millet system in the nineteenth-century Ottoman Empire. *The Muslim World, 57*(3), 212–223.

Kanovsky, E. (1986). Migration from the poor to the rich Arab countries. *Middle East Review, 18*(3), 28–36.

Keller, N. H. M., trans. (1994). Reliance of the Traveller A Classic Manual of Islamic Sacred law by Ibn Naqib Misri. Evanston, IL: Sunna Books.

Kyriakos, M. (1911). *Copts and Muslims under British control (Egypt)*. London: Smith, Elder and Co.

Lewis, B. (1984). *The Jews of Islam*. Princeton: Princeton University Press.

Lewis, B., & Churchill, B. E. (2009). *Islam the religion and the people*. Upper Saddle River: Wharton School Publishing.

Louer, L. (2008). *Transnational Shia politics. Religious and political networks in the Gulf*. New York: Columbia University Press.

Masters, B. (2001). *Christians and Jews in Ottoman Arab world: The roots of Sectarianism*. New York: Cambridge University Press.

Meinardus, O. F. A. (2002). *Coptic saints and pilgrimages*. Cairo: The American University in Cairo Press.

Minority Rights Group International. (2010). State of the World's Minorities and Indigenous Peoples 2010. *Egypt*. London: Minority Rights Group International. Retrieved from http://www.minorityrights.org/3937/egypt/egypt-overview.html. Accessed 2 Nov 2011.

Minority Rights Group International. (2011a). *Lebanon*. London: Minority Rights Group International. Retrieved from http://www.minorityrights.org/5058/lebanon/lebanon-overview.html. Accessed 2 Nov 2011.

Minority Rights Group International. (2011b). *Saudi Arabia*. London: Minority Rights Group International. Retrieved from http://www.minorityrights.org/4302/saudi-arabia/saudi-arabia-overview.html. Accessed 2 Nov 2011.

Mouassaoui, R. (2011). Lebanon youths revolt against confessional system. *AFP News*, 24 Feb. Retrieved from www.lebnews.net/feb-2011-archive.html.

Nasr, V. (2006). *The Shia revival: How conflicts within Islam will shape the future*. New York: W. Norton & Company.

Norton, A. R. (1991). Lebanon after Taif: Is the civil war over? *Middle East Journal, 45*(3), 466.

Onwudiwe, I. D. (2006). Egypt. In D. K. Das (Ed.), *World encyclopedia of police* (Vol. 1, pp. 259–262). Routledge: New York.

Palestinian Human Rights Organization. (2011). *Camp in fear, camp in want human*.

Rougier, B. (2008). Fatah al-Islam: un réseau jihadiste au coeur des contradictions libanaises. In B. Rougier (Ed.), *Qu'est ce que le Salafisme*. Paris: PUF.

Tolefson, H. (1999). *Policing Islam: The British occupation of Egypt and the Anglo-Egyptian struggle over control of the police, 1882–1914*. Westport: Greenwood.

U.S. Department of State. (2009). *International religious freedom report*. Bureau of Democracy, Human Rights, and Labor. 26 Oct, 2009. Retrieved from http://www.state.gov/g/drl/rls/irf/2009/127357.htm.

United Nations Relief and Works Agency. (2008). A common challenge a shared responsibility. New York: United Nations Relief and Works Agency. 23 June 2008. Retrieved from http://www.unrwa.org/userfiles/201001193369.pdf.

Varghese, J. (2010). Police structure: A comparative study of policing models. *Social Science Research Network*. Retrieved from http://ssrn.com/abstract=1605290 or http://dx.doi.org/10.2139/ssrn.1605290. Accessed 2 Nov 2011.

Chapter 8
Policing Muslims in a "Combat/Peace" Environment: The Case of "Policing by Religion" in Israel

Qasim Haq and M.R. Haberfeld

Muslim Communities and "Policing by Religion"

In the decade following 9/11, Muslim communities in the West have been placed under high scrutiny. Prior to 9/11, police engagement with Muslim communities was virtually nonexistent due to the normative focus on "racial" and "ethnic" identities, as opposed to religious ones, a trend emulated in criminal justice research and social policy with religion as a focal point (Spalek et al. 2009). Chakraborti (2007, p. 109) points out a twofold relationship between the police and the Muslim community: "the threat posed *to* Muslims as targets of racially and religiously motivated prejudice and *by* Muslims as potential sources of 'terror' and scourges of national security." The dual roles for local police include protecting the local Muslim community from hate crime, while at the same time defending the state from those within the community who pose a terrorist threat. The balance between the two is delicate and easier stated than drawn.

Drawing on the post-9/11 American-Muslim experiences and the case of policing Catholic minorities in Northern Ireland, the authors highlight policing of the Muslim community in Israel. In the aftermath of the 1967 Six Days War in Israel, Israel Police response to policing Muslim communities entered a "Combat/Peace" mindset, a mindset that has not changed for more than four decades. The importance of this chapter lies on one end in the way certain Muslim communities are being policed in the twenty-first century in the United States, in a way that raises many concerns as it parallels the failed approach of the Israeli Police, and on the other end, in the ability to look at different environments that embarked, originally, on the misguided way of "policing by religion," like the Royal Ulster Constabulary of Northern Ireland, but were able to later rethink and reform in a more effective manner. The danger of not learning from these policing histories is highlighted as a warning for the future of policing Muslim communities.

The "Combat/Peace" environments are operationalized by the authors as environments where certain religious communities are policed in a focused manner solely due to their religious affiliations, and the perceptions that they constitute a

F.B. Hakeem et al., *Policing Muslim Communities: Comparative International Context*, 117
DOI 10.1007/978-1-4614-3552-5_8, © Springer Science+Business Media New York 2012

legitimate threat to the larger society that is either explicitly or implicitly engaged in a state of combat, either an active state of war or the fragile peace in the aftermath. This state of "Combat/Peace" environments can also be present without the actual state of war in a given geographic location but can, by extension, be applied to countries such as the United States and United Kingdom that are engaged in warfare on foreign lands but experience the terrorist threat within the country as a response to their foreign warfare engagements.

American-Muslims and the 9/11 Aftermath

September 11 and its aftermath have brought many challenges for Muslims in the West. Life has become difficult for a majority of American-Muslims following 9/11 (PEW Research Center 2007). Moral panic about Islam has accelerated the process of what Werbner (2004) describes as the "spiraling progressive alienation" of Muslims in the West. Many Muslims feel alienated from the very communities to which they once belonged. Some avoid routine activities such as going out in the evenings, whereas businesses suspect that former customers avoid their firms (see Gaskew 2009 for an ethnographic account). Verbal and physical bias attacks against Muslims (Council on American-Islamic Relations 2008); those perceived to be Muslims (Chrisafis 2001); revenge murders (Spalek 2002); vandalism of mosques (Goodstein 2010); and the stabbing of a New York City cab driver amidst the Park 51 Muslim Community Center debate (Kleinfield 2010) are examples of such hardships. There has also been simultaneous growth in "faith-hate" and far-right activity directed against Muslims (McGhee 2005).

However, it is important to note that negative representations of Muslims and Islam in the West have historical roots that long predate the events of 9/11. The introduction of the term "Islamophobia" dates back to 1997 with the publication of *Islamophobia: A Challenge for Us All* by U.K.-based research institute, the Runnymede Trust (1997). Islamophobia "refers to unfounded hostility towards Islam. The term refers also to the practical consequences of such hostility that can be observed in unfair discrimination against Muslim individuals and communities, and the exclusion of Muslims from mainstream political and social affairs" (Runnymede Trust 1997, p. 4). The report notes a particular dramatic aspect of social exclusion, vulnerability to physical violence, and harassment of Muslims, that resulted in their being unable to play a full part in mainstream society. According to the Runnymede Trust (1997, p. 4),

> The term "Islamophobia" has been coined because there is a new reality which needs naming: anti-Muslim prejudice has grown so considerably and rapidly in recent years that a new item in the vocabulary is needed so that it can be identified and acted against. In a similar way there was a time in European history when a new word, anti-Semitism, was needed and coined to highlight the growing dangers of anti-Jewish hostility.

Islamophobia is not exclusively connected to the 9/11 attacks or the recent wars in Afghanistan and Iraq. But these events seem to have exacerbated Islamophobia. Researchers and public health workers point out the double burden faced by many

Muslims in Western countries, who not only suffer immense sadness at the death and destruction caused by terrorism, but must also live with the fear of increased stigma and discrimination (Khalid 2007; Inayat 2002; Bryan 2009; Yasmeen 2011). Barkdull et al. (2011) in research on experiences of Muslims in Argentina, Australia, Canada, and the United States call upon the social work profession to take a leadership role in addressing the stigmatization of Muslims.

Hickman and Walter (1997) draw parallels in the experience of Muslims in the West after 9/11, with that of the Irish in Great Britain following bombings of Irish targets (see also LeMay 2005, for comparisons to the German- and Japanese-American experience during World War II). Anyone who was Irish, had Irish relatives or friends, or any connection to Ireland, became a suspect. The impact of anti-terror legislation on people's lives in Britain created "suspect communities," where simple looks, accents, or a passport sometimes gave rise to suspicion in the minds of the police (see Hillyard 1993, the only ethnographic account of its kind). Hillyard (2005) suggests that such arbitrary and draconian measures can alienate the very communities from which the police require good intelligence.

Police Engagement with Muslim Communities

In addition to protecting citizens of the Muslim faith from hate crime, the police also must defend the State from terrorist threat. This means an evolutionary role for the local police. According to Oliver (2006), 9/11 was the beginning of a new era in policing, the *homeland security era*. The authorization of this era has largely come from the national and international threat of terrorism, driven by the events of 9/11. The era entails a centralized decision-making process, but the actual execution of the organization will, like the *community era*, entail a decentralized and flexible approach. The internal information sharing will feed the centralized decision-making, but it is the officer on the street who will execute these decisions with the flexibility of street-level decision making.

The July 7, 2005 London attacks by four British Muslims brought home the threat of homegrown terrorism and radicalization. This event brought closer to home the internal (local) nature of radicalization, once thought of as external (international), that alienated youths in Western societies are vulnerable to influence and recruitment by radical extremists. Kundnani (2002) notes that since the Bosnian Muslim genocide by Bosnian Serb forces in the early 1990s, growing numbers of youth have been attracted to more puritanical strands of Islam. This growing attraction is found among some sections of Muslim youth disenchanted with what they see as the subordination of Muslims across the world, and with their own experiences of social and political marginalization, and alienation (Atran 2010; Sageman 2008; Sivanandan 2006). The London 2005 attacks, along with 9/11, have resulted in an increased engagement between the local police and Muslim communities. The importance of engagement with communities to secure the State, better police–community relations, while gaining human intelligence in the process, is now viewed as being central to counterterrorism success, under the precept of "communities defeat terrorism" (Briggs et al. 2006, p. 83).

Counterterrorism policies and practices have been dominated by "hard-power" strategies involving surveillance, intelligence gathering, the use of informants, and the implementation of a number of anti-terror laws (Spalek et al. 2009). Previous research has established that trust and confidence in police can be seriously undermined in situations where communities feel that they are being over-policed (Macpherson Inquiry 1999; Jones and Newburn 2001; Tyler et al. 2010). This can have serious consequences upon the flow of information from communities (Hillyard 2005). According to Innes (2005, 2006), "soft-power" policing with consultation schemes between the police and Muslim communities can trigger an improvement in their relationship. "Soft" policing gives Muslim communities a greater opportunity to present their concerns and vulnerabilities to the police, while simultaneously generating intelligence opportunities for the police.

An example of one such scheme is the Muslim Contact Unit (MCU). Originated in the London Metropolitan Police, MCUs can today be found in police forces across the United Kingdom. MCUs are intelligence units with dual roles of protecting Muslim communities from Islamophobic abuse and assault, and gathering "community-by-community" intelligence on extremist activity (Dodd 2005). This bottom-up community engagement scheme attempts to identify extremism within Muslim communities through partnership with the law-abiding Muslim communities at large. MCUs count reclaiming a mosque from hard-core violent extremists, enhanced trust in policing through victim support in racist and Islamophobic attacks, and introduction of Muslim police officers into counterterrorism policing among its successes (Spalek et al. 2009, p. 47).

The NYPD has implemented various community-oriented programs to engage with the city's diverse Muslim communities. The police department is using sports competitions to build trust and engage with Muslim youths. The department has seen progress in engaging with the mainly Muslim Arabic-speaking communities through the NYPD Youth Soccer League. Encouraged by this success, the department devised the NYPD Cricket League while struggling to reach youths in the South Asian and West Indian communities. According to Deputy Inspector Amin Kosseim, "His [NYPD Commissioner Raymond Kelly] concept is the three Cs – crime fighting, counterterrorism, and community relations – and this is the community relations side. Playing cricket – It's a bond for the future" (Davies 2009). Youths aged between 14 and 19 from the Pakistani, Bangladeshi, and West Indian communities are recruited to join the program. In 2008 there were 6 teams and 100 players, in 2009 the participation grew to 10 teams and 170 players, including 2 girls, and are expected to grow next year (Davies 2009; NYPD Cricket 2008).

Local police authorities after 9/11 are undergoing a steep learning curve in relation to understanding and working with their local Muslim communities. Policing diversity now no longer solely calls for race and gender to be considered; religion is also important (Stout 2010). Law enforcement agencies today provide their employees with sensitivity training on dealing with different religious communities.

Practical matters such as taking shoes off before entering a mosque, not shaking hands with a person of the opposite sex, eye contact, and so on, are all points of discussion in local police precincts (Navarro 2002; Stainbrook 2010).

Therefore, the news exposed by the Associated Press in 2011, about the existence of the NYPD's Moroccan Initiative and Demographic Unit was a rude awakening for Muslim communities and policing scholars alike. Under the "Moroccan Initiative" the NYPD subjected entire neighborhoods of American-Moroccans (U.S. citizens and recent immigrants) to surveillance and scrutiny because of the ethnicity of the residents, not because of any accusations of crimes. The Demographic Unit, the existence of which was denied by the NYPD at first, dispatched undercover officers into minority neighborhoods as part of a human mapping program (Associated Press 2011). Yet, focusing NYPD's surveillance efforts on Muslim communities is nothing new in the history of democratic policing. The case of "policing by religion" can be traced, among others, to Northern Ireland and Israel. In the case of the former, "policing by religion" was not focused on the Muslim religion but rather on the Catholic religion, and in the latter it was the Muslim religion that became the focal point of a certain police strategy. Regardless of what religion one is looking at, the idea of "policing by religion" appears to have an apprehensive connotation to put it as mildly as possible.

Religion and Policing: The Case of Northern Ireland

Policing in Northern Ireland brings to light the drastic interface of religion and policing. The Northern Ireland conflict caused by political divisions, economic devastation, and social polarization, found policing as a major source of contention. Since its independence in 1921, Northern Ireland police had the responsibility for both policing the community and maintaining the state. The Royal Ulster Constabulary (RUC) held very different meaning for the Protestant and the Catholic communities. Police were largely supported by the Protestant Unionist and Loyalists communities, but opposed by the Catholic Nationalist and Republican communities. Protestants viewed the RUC as a necessary protector against the aggression of Republicans, while the Catholics viewed it as a representation of a discriminatory state (Mulcahy 2006; Stout 2010).

The RUC was overwhelmingly Protestant throughout its history, despite the fact that one-third of the population of Northern Ireland identified as Catholics. Protestant and Catholic communities' attitudes were divided on a range of political and social issues, divisions that seeped into the police force. Augusteijn's (2007) *The Memoirs of John M Regan* presents a rare autobiographical account of a Catholic officer in the RUC, John M. Regan. The book offers an insight into the grievances and alienation experienced by Regan, a moderate Catholic officer in a majority Protestant police force. Regan claimed "The question of a man's religion had no bearing whatever on his prospect of promotion" (Augusteijn 2007, p. 191). McGarry (2009) suggests that Regan's testimony, at times, underplays sectarianism and discrimination to the point of self-deception as Regan later claims that he was passed over for the post of Belfast police commissioner due to his religion (Augusteijn 2007, pp. 212–213).

The RUC was often criticized for impartial policing practices towards the religious minority Catholic communities. Major scandals rocked the RUC. Officers sometimes confirmed that there were firm grounds to these allegations. An undercover RUC officer interviewed by Ellison and Smyth (1995) had no doubt that high-level clearance had been given for the killing of citizens who were considered paramilitary suspects. The Patten Commission (1999, p. 81) set up to consider the future of policing in Northern Ireland made several recommendations, stating: "The police service should be representative of the society it polices." For the police to be religiously representative of the state, it was recommended that there should be a 50:50 recruitment of Catholics and Protestants for 10 years, with the aim that at the end of that period, the police service should be 30% Catholic (Stout 2010, p. 113).

The RUC, renamed the Police Service of Northern Ireland (PSNI), has seen vast changes in its evolution following the Patten Commission inquiry. The Patten Commission (1999) recommended a 50:50 recruitment policy as a means of making the police service representative of the community. The 50:50 provision was applied only to the constable level. The purpose of the 50:50 provision was to effect compositional change in terms of religion. This is best done at the constable level, where recruitment takes place in large numbers (Northern Ireland Policing Board n.d.).

The Catholic composition of the RUC stood at 8.28% at the time of the Patten Commission inquiry (1999). The temporary provision aimed to increase Catholics in the police force to a 30% level, in lieu with the one-third of the population of Northern Ireland that identified as Catholics. The pie charts in Fig. 8.1 illustrate the change in PSNI composition over a 10-year period. Figure 8.1 illustrates PSNI composition as of November 1, 2001, before the introduction of the temporary 50:50 provision (Northern Ireland Office 2009). Figure 8.2 illustrates the most recent PSNI data. PSNI Catholic composition stands at 30.32% today (Police Service of Northern Ireland 2011).

The Patten Commission's 50:50 provision has been successful in changing the PSNI workforce composition. Having reached the 30% Catholic representation, the Northern Ireland Government allowed the 50:50 provision to lapse in March 2011. Plans for future police recruitment are currently under consideration by the government (Northern Ireland Policing Board n.d.).

Public trust in the police also seems to have increased as PSNI has become more representative of its community. The Northern Ireland Crime Survey indicates that public trust in the police is on the rise. A 10.7% increase from 72% in 2003–2004 to 82.7% in 2010–2011 is noted when asked, "Police treat Catholics and Protestants the same in Northern Ireland as a whole" (U.K. Department of Justice 2011, p. 1). Changes have also taken hold in gender and ethnic minority composition of the PSNI workforce. Such changes not advocated directly by the 50:50 provision are perhaps a by-product of recruitment policies aimed at diversifying the police force. PSNI female composition has changed from 12.68% in 2001 to 24.58% in 2011. This is significant itself as PSNI now has one of the world's highest ratios of female

Fig. 8.1 Royal Ulster
Constabulary religious
composition as of November
2001, before the 50:50 Patten
Commission provision
(Northern Ireland Office
2009)

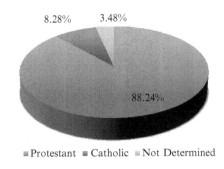

8.28%   3.48%

88.24%

■ Protestant ■ Catholic ■ Not Determined

Fig. 8.2 Police Service
of Northern Ireland religious
composition as of November
2011, 10 years since the
50:50 Patten Commission
provision (Police Service
of Northern Ireland 2011)

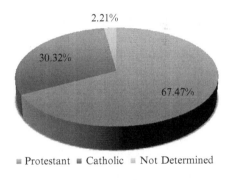

2.21%

30.32%

67.47%

■ Protestant ■ Catholic ■ Not Determined

police officers (Northern Ireland Human Rights Commission 2010). The ethnic minority police composition of 0.48% today represents the 0.48% ethnic composition of Northern Ireland population at large (Police Service of Northern Ireland 2011; Northern Ireland Office 2009).

Northern Ireland, as an example, is used here to suggest the drastic impact of religion on policing. The RUC is unique as many other factors are at play, including the dual roles of police to protect citizens and the state, controlling crime as well as violence caused by nationalist aspirations. The case of John M. Regan presents an interesting insight into the experience of a religious minority police officer. It is plausible that influenced by the police subculture, Regan first and foremost identified as a police officer, hence at times overlooking the inequalities of a majority Protestant police force. In his research with RUC officers, Mapstone (1992) records the experiences of Catholic police officers. It is noted that friendship patterns among officers emulate the wider community divide, and Catholics have to detach themselves from the wider Catholic community when joining the police force (Mapstone 1992). The Patten Commission (1999) recommendation of creating a police service representative of the state does suggest that although otherwise a secular institution, religion can have a profound influence in policing practices, police engagement with religious groups, police–community relations, hiring practices, and the legitimacy of police in the eyes of the citizenry.

Policing Muslims in the "Peace/Combat" Environment: The Case of Israel

Since its inception in 1948, the Israel National Police (INP) has been a highly centralized national force, under the responsibility of the minister of public security (formerly called "the ministry of police"). After the Six Days War (1967), Israeli state territory expanded and terrorist activity within Israel escalated reaching new peaks, with simultaneous attacks on the Israeli targets aboard. Consequently the IP reorganized its outreach to include east Jerusalem, Judea, Samaria, Gaza Strip, Sinai Peninsula, and the Golan Heights. In addition, organizational adjustments in the structure of the Border Guard Police took place to respond to the increased threat of terrorism. In the Judea and Samaria territories new police jurisdictions were formed under the supervision of military governors to address issues of law enforcement and to provide police services to the population (Gideon and Geva 2007).

In the mid to late 1970s Israel came under much pressure to respond in a more effective manner to the numerous terrorist attacks and attempted attacks within the major cities, especially the city of Jerusalem. The IP addressed these growing threats by creating and/or revamping a number of specialized units aimed at targeting terrorism-related issues. It came as no surprise that the focus of these units' activity was solely skewed towards the Muslim population of Israel, be it the residents of the territories that became part of Israel after the Six Days War, or "Israeli Arabs," meaning the Arab population that lived within the borders of Israel, as defined prior to the war. Not all of the Israeli Arabs are of the Muslim religion but the primary focus of police attention was devoted to the Muslims (Haberfeld, field notes 2011).

Data from the Central Bureau of Statistics (2011) indicates that Israel's Arab population numbers approximately 1,587,000 residents, 20.5% of the national population. The Israeli Arab population includes a number of different religious and ethnic groups, including a large number of Christians and Druze. Muslims, however, are the dominant religious group. Muslims constitute almost 83% of the Israeli-Arab composition. Israeli Arabs are Israeli citizens, but have strong national, religious, and familial ties and contacts with Arabs in the Palestinian territories from where most of the terrorist attacks have originated (Hasisi et al. 2011).

The unchallenged perception of the 1970s that led to the creation of the new units was that all terrorist activity directed against Israel was only perpetrated by the Muslim minority. The two units most active within the IP were the "Minorities Unit" or "Michlak Miutim" (in Hebrew), and a specialized military unit called "Soldier in the Service of the Police" or in short "HIBA" (based on the Hebrew acronym of its full name). The main purpose of these units was to deal with the "problems" of terrorism. In addition, within various investigative units, for example, the investigation division, a number of police officers from the minority background, be it Muslims or members of other minority religion, were assigned to deal with the "problems" generated by the Muslim minority communities (Haberfeld, field notes 2011).

One of the authors of this chapter was assigned to serve first in the HIBA during her service with the Israel Defense Forces, and later as a member of the Israel Police in the Juvenile Investigative Bureau for the city of Jerusalem. The Juvenile Investigative Bureau comprised six teams, one of which was referred to as the Minority Team. The following account is based on the author's recollection of "policing by religion." Policing by religion appears, from the perspective of time and other developments, as one of the factors associated with increased numbers of terrorist activity that plagued and continues to challenge Israeli society for the past four decades.

The initial training for the members of specialized unit HIBA did not include any modules about sensitivity towards the Muslim population, the group HIBA soldiers were about to police. The bulk of the training focused on use of force, self-defense, martial arts techniques, and the identification of explosives. Endless hours of training were devoted to familiarize the recruits with terrorists' tactics, from letters containing explosive devices to identification of suspicious individuals, and objects placed on the streets in various urban environments. Not a word was allocated to the possibility that one day the soldiers may encounter an Israeli Jew who will smuggle a suitcase of explosives into the city of Jerusalem. The total and complete focus of the counterterrorism training was on one, very specific segment of the Israeli society, the Muslims. A few years later, when an Israeli Jew was caught with his suitcase filled with explosives the author recalls the ignorance of the trainers, and the tactical error of focusing on a religious group instead of the intent and incentives to commit a crime.

What the author and her colleagues were trained were a host of tactics yet the sensitivity training was missing. This error of judgment by the IP trainer resulted in a misguided approach towards the Muslim community, which generated disdain towards an entire group, and led to verbal and sometimes use of excessive physical force. The granted assumption that HIBA members will be dealing with "the enemy" each time they encounter someone of the Muslim faith created a dangerous and counterproductive indoctrination that took years to shake off. Such an assumption went beyond the level of social and human error, and led to failure at the tactical level. This tactical error made HIBA members overlook the Jewish terrorist, and years later made the bodyguards of Prime Minister Yitzchak Rabin miss the Jewish extremist who murdered him in broad daylight.

The second encounter with policing by religion while in the service of the Israel National Police was the author's experience in policing with the Minority Team within the Jerusalem Juvenile Bureau. The Minority Team was composed of two Israeli Arabs of Muslim religion who were born in Jordan and lived in East Jerusalem that became part of the State of Israel after the Six Days War, and two Druze officers, originally from the Golan Heights. While the author was not assigned to the Minority Team, it was quite frequent that she was assigned to police with the Minority Team when the team membership was periodically depleted of its permanent members due to other policing related tasks. It was during these days and weeks that the author was exposed for the first time to "sensitivity training." Although completely informal and delivered via the nature of her police tasks, this "on-the-job" sensitivity training was the defining moment in her understanding of what was missing in the original counterterrorism training.

The understanding of a culture, the nuances, and sensitivity in dealing with a religious minority group, were missing from the original training of HIBA. This led, more often than not, to escalation in police–public encounters, and reinforcement of negative stereotypes rather than effective policing. The understanding of the subjects of focused policing from the humanized rather than a dehumanized angle made all the difference. Yet, the damage of the early years of indoctrination was already done. Lack of sensitivity training not only emboldens biased policing practices, but also generates animosity among the minority groups who perceive the police as unjust. It is plausible that such policing biases may help create more terrorists then solve the terrorist "problem."

Today (2011), and for a number of years already, the Israel National Police has addressed this very complex issue of minority policing via different modules of training. A glance at the training curricula of the IP shows various sensitivity training modules directed at various levels of police personnel, from the basic to the more advanced officers' training. The modules include examples from other countries, including the United States and the infamous Los Angeles Police Department's struggles with racial/sensitivity-related issues, as well as a much more specific set of guidelines for dealing with the Arab minority in Israel on a local/station-level of engagement (The Abraham Fund Initiative 2011).

The critical issue, however, is more complex than inclusion or lack of sensitivity training. There is much concern and not enough empirical research to suggest the operational effectiveness and sanity of a tactical approach that mandates the creation of "minority units" that focus the majority of their attention, as in the case of Israel, on a religious minority, equating, de facto, religious affiliation with a perceived propensity towards a certain criminal activity, that is, the act of terrorism. If there are any preconceived notions in the history of policing that one would want to see vanish and disappear forever, it is what we refer to as "policing by religion."

Although the height of terrorist activity against Israel took place in the years 2006 and 2007, over three decades after these accounts, it is hypothesized that the creation of specialized units to police by religion was and is a somewhat research-worthy contribution to understand better the acceleration of the terrorist phenomenon in Israel and to its possible minimization in the future.

Policing as if We Are All Equal: Lessons We Can Learn but Do We Want to?

A cursory glance at the police practices of engagement with minority religious communities in Northern Ireland, United States, United Kingdom, and Israel can be called "policing by religion." This concept can provide the scholars of democratic policing with insight into the trajectories of unsuccessful versus successful operational approaches to a very specific aspect of what can be a modality of problem-oriented policing. The need, real or perceived, to police certain religious groups within the community at large that denotes an existence of a "problem" falls within the realm of what policing scholars have referred to for decades as problem-oriented policing. Such an approach, that equates one's religious affiliation with creating problems for the larger community is a recipe for disaster. Furthermore, this recipe for disaster spans across and beyond what a local group of problematic individuals can do to endanger the others.

Lessons learned from the experience of nations discussed in this chapter point to one clear direction. Radicalization of passive supporters of the cause, whatever the cause may be, can be very well achieved by signaling to the community at large that the problem can possibly be or indeed is associated with one's religious beliefs, rather than one's propensity towards criminal behavior. Criminologists, for generations, have attributed individual and collective predisposition to criminal behavior based on a host of physiological, psychological, economic, environmental, and sociological factors, among other variables. Police organizations around the world, however, tend to disregard hundreds of years of research, and rationalize their operational priorities based on a testimonial rather than empirical findings.

Based on the most recent information available on the website from the Israeli police, it is composed of seven main branches and nine units that are not branch affiliated. The districts, regions, and stations are responsible for delivering police services within six territorial districts. Each district has its regions and stations that are subordinate to the district. The region represents a subunit of the district, which is designed to function as an independent basic police unit responsible for the delivery of police services within its territorial jurisdiction. The station is a subunit of the district or the region, and is designed to function as an independent basic police unit responsible for the delivery of the basic police services within its territorial jurisdiction. A new, state-of-the-art training center has been created in 2011 that will afford the IP with a host of technologically advanced training opportunities (Israel Police n.d.).

Yet, despite these clearly advanced steps in the training arena, and the fact that the IP is structurally advanced to serve its geographically distributed Muslim minority populations that can be found in each and every district, region, and station the soundness of the existence of a minority unit can and should still be challenged, as a valid form of democratic policing.

The perceptions of the community, political pressures, and individual understandings, or lack thereof, replace scientific evidence that refutes legitimacy of the policing by religion model. For Israel, the concept of policing in a "combat/peace" environment can be approached and modified based on the model adopted by the Police Service of Northern Ireland (PSNI). As noted above, the Patten Commission's (1999) 50:50 temporary provision was devised to reflect the approximately 30% Catholic population of Northern Ireland. The purpose of the 50:50 provision was to make the police service representative of the community. As Israel's Arab population (Muslim and non-Muslim) constitutes just over the 20% mark in the year 2012, maybe an 80:20 provision could be considered instead of the existing "minority units." An 80:20 provision in Israel can attempt to diversify the police force, make the police service representative of the community, rule out the need for minority units, and make the IP a democratic policing model. On the other hand, the NYPD's efforts to map the Muslim communities of New York City and the Moroccan Initiative seem to be invalid and counterproductive as police tactics. The efforts of the NYPD to diversify its ranks did not focus on the religious affiliation but rather race, gender, and sexual orientation. It is plausible that directing the diversity efforts primarily towards religious affiliation would eliminate the need for such a misguided approach. Furthermore, creating the Muslim Contact Unit within the London Metropolitan Police force does not appear to offer the desired departure solution from labeling certain minorities as "problematic" or "others."

Nonetheless, the final words of this chapter call for a more comprehensive study of the combat/peace environments in which members of certain religious group are treated as the "others." The research question for the future remains: policing as if we are all equal is a worthy, human rights-rooted concept; there are lessons from the past that we can learn but, seriously, do we want to?

References

Abraham Fund Initiatives. (2011). Available at http://www.abrahamfund.org.

Associated Press. (2011). *Highlights of AP's probe into NYPD intelligence operations*. http://ap.org/nypd/. Accessed 12 Feb 2011.

Atran, S. (2010). *Talking to the enemy: Faith, brotherhood, and the (un)making of terrorists*. New York: Harper Collins.

Augusteijn, J. (Ed.). (2007). *The memoirs of John M Regan: A catholic officer in the RIC and RUC, 1909–48*. Dublin: Four Courts Press.

Barkdull, C., Khaja, K., Queiro-Tajalli, I., Swart, A., Cunningham, D., & Dennis, S. (2011). Experiences of Muslims in four Western countries post – 9/11. *Journal of Women and Social Work, 26*(2), 139–153.

Briggs, R., Fieschi, C., & Lownsbrough, H. (2006). *Bringing it home: Community-based approaches to counter-terrorism*. London: Demos.

Bryan, J. L. (2009). *Terror town: The impact of 9/11 on Arab Muslims, intergroup relationships and community life in Jersey City*. Unpublished dissertation, Yale University, New Haven.

Central Bureau of Statistics. (2011, May 8). *63rd Independence Day – Approximately 7,746,000 residents in the State of Israel*. http://www1.cbs.gov.il/www/hodaot2011n/11_11_101e.pdf. Retrieved 12 Feb 2012.

Chakraborti, N. (2007). Policing Muslim communities. In M. Rowe (Ed.), *Policing beyond Macpherson* (pp. 107–127). Portland: Willan Publishing.

Chrisafis, A. (2001, Oct 12). Muslims in Britain urged to back jihad of peace. *The Guardian*. http://www.guardian.co.uk/uk/2001/oct/12/september11.afghanistan. Retrieved 23 Nov 2011.

Council on American-Islamic Relations. (2008). *The status of Muslim civil rights in the United States: 2008*. http://www.cair.com/Portals/0/pdf/civilrights2008.pdf. Retrieved 28 Nov 2011.

Davies, A. (2009, July 27). Bouncers in Brooklyn as NYPD pitches up community cricket. *Sydney Morning Herald*. http://www.smh.com.au/news/sport/cricket/bouncers-in-brooklyn-as-nypd-pitches-up-community-cricket/2009/07/26/1248546631055.html. Retrieved 21 Mar 2010.

Dodd, V. (2005, July 19). Special branch to track Muslims across UK. *The Guardian*. http://www.guardian.co.uk/uk/2005/jul/20/religion.july7. Retrieved 14 Jan 2012.

Ellison, G., & Smyth, J. (1995). Bad apples or rotten barrels? In O. Marenin (Ed.), *Policing change, changing police: International perspectives*. New York: Garland.

Gaskew, T. (2009). Peacemaking criminology and counterterrorism: Muslim Americans and the war on terror. *Contemporary Justice Review, 12*(3), 345–366.

Gideon, L., & Geva, R. (2007). Policing under fire: The constant change of allocation of resources in the Israeli police. In M. R. Haberfeld & I. Cerrah (Eds.), *Comparative policing: The struggle for democratization*. Thousand Oaks: Sage.

Goodstein, L. (2010, Sept 5). American Muslims ask, will we ever belong? *The New York Times*. http://www.nytimes.com/2010/09/06/us/06muslims.html. Retrieved 17 Oct 2011.

Haberfeld, M. R. (2011). Field notes.

Hasisi, B., Alpert, G. P., & Flynn, D. (2011). The impacts of policing terrorism on society: Lessons from Israel and the U.S. In D. Weisburd, T. Feucht, I. Hakimi, M. Lois, & S. Perry (Eds.), *To protect and to serve: Policing in the years of terrorism, and beyond*. New York: Springer.

Hickman, M. J., & Walter, B. (1997). *Discrimination and the Irish community in Britain*. London: Commission for Racial Equality.

Hillyard, P. (1993). *Suspect community: Peoples experience of the prevention of terrorism acts in Britain*. Boulder: Pluto.

Hillyard, P. (2005). *The "War on Terror:" Lessons from Ireland*. European Civil Liberties Network. http://www.ecln.org/essays/essay-1.pdf. Retrieved 23 Mar 2011.

Inayat, Q. (2002). The meaning of being a Muslim: An aftermath of the twin towers episode. *Counseling Psychology Quarterly, 15*(4), 351–358.

Innes, M. (2005). Why 'soft' policing is hard: On the curious development of reassurance policing, how it became neighbourhood policing and what this signifies about the politics of police reform. *Journal of Community and Applied Social Psychology, 15*, 156–169.

Innes, M. (2006). Policing uncertainty: Countering terror through community intelligence and democratic policing. *Annals of American Academy of Political and Social Science, 605*, 222–241.

Israel Police. (n.d.). http://www.police.gov.il/english/AboutPolice/Pages/default.aspx. Retrieved 13 Feb 2012.

Jones, T., & Newburn, T. (2001). *Widening access: Improving police relations with hard to reach groups*. Police research series paper 138. London: Home Office. http://library.npia.police.uk/docs/hopolicers/prs138bn.pdf. Accessed 25 Jan 2012.

Khalid, S. (2007). Counseling from an Islamic perspective. *Therapy Today, 18*, 34–37.

Kleinfield, N. R. (2010, Aug 25). Rider asks if cabby is Muslim, then stabs him. *The New York Times*. http://www.nytimes.com/2010/08/26/nyregion/26cabby.html?pagewanted=all. Retrieved 17 Oct 2011.

Kundnani, A. (2002). An unholy alliance? Racism, religion, and communalism. *Race & Class, 44*(2), 71–80.

LeMay, M. C. (2005). *The perennial struggle: Race, ethnicity, and minority group relations in the United States* (2nd ed.). Upper Saddle River: Prentice-Hall.

Macpherson Inquiry. (1999). *The Stephen Lawrence inquiry: Report of an inquiry by Sir William Macpherson of Cluny*. (Cm 4262–I). London: Home Office.

Mapstone, R. (1992). The attitudes of police in a divided society: The case of Northern Ireland. *British Journal of Criminology, 32*(2), 183–192.

McGarry, F. (2009). The memoirs of John M Regan: A catholic officer in the RIC and RUC, 1909–48. [Review of the book *The memoirs of John M Regan: A catholic officer in the RIC and RUC, 1909–48*, by J. Augusteijn]. *English Historical Review, 510*, 1202–1204.

McGhee, D. (2005). *Intolerant Britain? Hate, citizenship, and difference*. Berkshire: McGraw Hill Education.

Mulcahy, A. (2006). *Policing Northern Ireland: Conflict, legitimacy and reform*. Portland: Willan Publishing.

Navarro, J. (2002). Interacting with Arabs and Muslims. *FBI Law Enforcement Bulletin, 71*(9), 20–23.

Northern Ireland Human Rights Commission. (2010). *Response on the Police (Northern Ireland) Act 2000: Review of temporary recruitment provisions*. Northern Ireland: Belfast.

Northern Ireland Office. (2009). *Police (Northern Ireland) Act 2000: Review of temporary recruitment provisions*. (Consultation Paper 1928091). Belfast: Northern Ireland Office.

Northern Ireland Policing Board. (n.d.). *Why was there a 50:50 recruitment policy?* http://www. nipolicingboard.org.uk/index/faqs/recruitment.htm. Retrieved 11 Feb 2011.

NYPD Cricket. (2008, July 22). *NYPD forms cricket league for New York City youth.* Retrieved from New York City Police Department website on 21 Mar 2010. http://www.nyc.gov/html/ nypd/html/pr/pr_2008_029.shtml.

Oliver, W. M. (2006). The fourth era of policing: Homeland security. *International Review of Law, Computers & Technology, 20*, 49–62.

Patten Commission. (1999). *A new beginning: Policing in Northern Ireland. The report of the independent on policing in Northern Ireland*. Belfast: Stationery Office.

PEW Research Center. (2007). *Muslim Americans: Middle class and mostly mainstream*. http:// pewresearch.org/assets/pdf/Muslim-americans.pdf. Retrieved 11 Oct 2011.

Police Service of Northern Ireland. (2011, Nov 1). *Workforce composition figures*. http://www. psni.police.uk/index/updates/updates_statistics/updates_workforce_composition_figures.htm. Retrieved 11 Feb 2011.

Sageman, M. (2008). *Leaderless Jihad: Terror networks in the twenty-first century*. Philadelphia: University of Pennsylvania Press.

Sivanandan, A. (2006). Race, terror and civil society. *Race & Class, 47*(3), 1–8.

Spalek, B. (Ed.). (2002). *Islam, crime, and criminal justice*. Portland: Willian Publishing.

Spalek, B., El Awa, S., & McDonald, L. Z. (2009). *Police-Muslim engagement and partnerships for the purposes of counter-terrorism: An examination*. Birmingham: University of Birmingham.

Stainbrook, M. G. (2010). Policing with Muslim communities in the age of terrorism. *The Police Chief, 77*, 32–40.

Stout, B. (2010). *Policing matters: Equality and diversity in policing*. Exeter: Learning Matters.

Trust, R. (1997). *Islamophobia: A challenge for us all*. London: The Runnymede Trust.

Tyler, T. R., Schulhofer, S., & Huq, A. Z. (2010). Legitimacy and deterrence effects in counterterrorism policing: A study of Muslim Americans. *Law and Society Review, 44*(2), 365–402.

U.K. Department of Justice. (2011). *Perceptions of policing, justice and anti-social behaviour: Quarterly update to September 2011*. (Statistics and Research Bulletin, 2). Belfast, Northern Ireland.

Werbner, P. (2004). The predicament of diaspora and millennial Islam: reflection on September 11, 2001. *Ethnicities, 4*(4), 451–476.

Yasmeen, S. (2011). Muslim minorities in the West: Spatially distant trauma. *Australia and New Zealand Journal of Public Health, 35*(4), 316.

Chapter 9
Conclusions: Pathways Towards an Equity and Parity in Policing

Looking at a Long Existing Problem and Creating Pathways Towards Solutions

The main goal of this book is to engage in and provoke a more intense and empirically grounded academic discourse on the effective and equitable form of policing of religious minority communities.

The book started with an in-depth look into the concepts of punishment under the sharia law and how they affect our perceptions and misperceptions of policing the Muslim communities.

From the ancient concepts a pathway is offered towards understanding of the ways policing of Muslim communities is conducted by modern Western democracies and provides a glimpse into the consequences of deeply rooted prejudice and biases and their impact on operational decisions within the progressive world of police decision makers.

The natural progression from the Western democracies and their focus on human rights is addressed in the chapter dealing with the concepts of human rights and the Islamic law, by demystifying the approach that leads to equating the Islamic law as antithetical to human rights which, in turn, leads to legitimization of stereotypes and suspicions.

As the pendulum swings based on the evidence of prejudice that mirrors more the medieval ages rather than the twenty-first century, we offer a glimpse into policing and the administration of justice in medieval India followed by policing in contemporary India which highlights the roots of the problems from the past and the consequences of policing in the present.

From a different angle policing minorities by the Muslim majority is also presented to underline the problems of religion-based policing or policing by religious-based precepts. The denial of concepts of equity and parity to different minorities in Muslim majority regions suggests that Islamic jurisprudence does not permit these concepts, which appears to be contrary to the Islamic religion that preaches equality

F.B. Hakeem et al., *Policing Muslim Communities: Comparative International Context*, 131
DOI 10.1007/978-1-4614-3552-5_9, © Springer Science+Business Media New York 2012

and nondiscrimination. Nonetheless, practices and police functions in countries ruled by the Muslim majority suggest otherwise and reinforce the perception that Islam mistreats followers of other religions. Such approaches to policing not only add fuel to already stereotyped understandings of the Muslim religion but also underscore the importance for these nations to implement police strategies that more closely adhere to the faith that stands for equity and parity. However, not all nations ruled by Muslim majorities reflect the practices of Saudi Arabia or Egypt. There are countries that adopted a different style of policing, one in which, at least from the official standpoint, there is a clear division between the pervasive influence of religion and professional policing.

More specifically, one good example of the separation between the civic duties of a police force and religion is the case of the Turkish National Police, the TNP. The following excerpt was contributed by Dr. Ibrahim Cerrah (2012).

Secularism and the Turkish National Police (TNP)

Despite the fact that Turkey is a predominantly Muslim nation it is ruled by a secular legal system. The laws, which the police are expected to enforce, are secular and not based on Islamic jurisdiction.

However, the Turkish version of secularism, compared to the Western countries, seems to be more strict and extreme. Police officers, Muslims or those belonging to any other religious denominations, are not officially allowed to practice their religious rituals while on duty. For instance, government officials are not allowed to wear clothing or symbols, which have religious meanings. Similarly, neither police officers nor any other civil servants are allowed, while on duty, to grow beard or put on hats *(kipa)* on their heads. Female police officers or other civil servants are not allowed to wear a *hijab (scarf)* covering their hair excluding the face.

On the other hand, some of the government practices are influenced or based on Islamic tradition. For example, two major Islamic rituals are officially accepted and celebrated as national holidays. These are *Ramadan*, the month of fasting, and *Kurban,* sacrificing an animal as a religious ritual. These two seasons are officially accepted and celebrated as national holidays. All civil service institutions such as the universities and other educational institutions, the police and even the military officially allow their members to have vacation and celebrate these festivals.

However, Muslims also have a compulsory weekly holiday on Fridays called *Cuma Prayer.* It is a religious obligation to all men to go to the mosque during noon time and join a prayer, which only lasts about an hour. While Saturday and Sundays are used as weekly holidays in Turkey, Friday is not officially accepted as the holiday of the week. Muslim police officers and other civil servants are not officially allowed to go to the mosque to perform this compulsory weekly prayer. However, as the Cuma prayers, which are performed in the middle of the day, coincides with the lunch break, most of the civil service institutions including the police tolerate or turns a blind eye to their members attending the *Cuma prayer*. On the other hand this is not a legally allowed or accepted practice. In other words, it is not a *de jure* but de facto practice.

Turkish police, in recent years, have been criticized by the extreme secular section of the Turkish society for being increasingly more religious and even sometime fundamentalist. However, this remains an unsubstantiated accusation as there is no empirical data supporting this. Research conducted on police sub culture shows that overwhelming majority, if not all, of the police officers are derived from lower middle and working class section of the Turkish society. This section of the society is predominantly conservative and holds strong religious beliefs and values. Religiosity of the Turkish Police officers can be seen as the natural manifestation of their class values, rather than being an increase in their religiosity. Yet, there is no evidence of police rendering a preferential treatment to criminals based on their religious affiliation. On the contrary, the police organization, in general, is quite tough and intolerant in their fight against crime committed by members of Islamic groups. Again, there is no evidence of police practice, which directly discriminates against the members of other religious ethnic minorities, in Turkey.

Policing with Parity and Equity

As the policing profession is sometimes compared to the medical one, it is hard to imagine that the followers of the Hippocratic Oath would ever consider creating specialized medical units to treat patients based on their religious affiliations. It is true that certain ethnic/racial groups are predisposed towards certain types of diseases and are studied as such but, nobody has ever scientifically proved, nor does there appear to be any movement in that direction, that people who practice one religion and suffer from an illness should be treated in a different manner than the ones who suffer from the same illness but practice another type of religion. A doctor suggesting that a Muslim patient suffering from high blood pressure should be treated in a different way than a Christian suffering from the same ailment would not only be ridiculed by his or her colleagues but probably, and justifiably so, also be barred from practicing the medical profession.

Yet, nobody seems to raise a hue and cry over focused police practices of religious minorities that are sometimes disguised as implemented to help rather than discriminate against the aforementioned minorities. A perfect example of such a disguise can be found in the British Muslim Contact Unit that was supposedly created to facilitate the understanding between the London Metropolitan police and the Muslim community but, in reality stigmatizes the population it is supposed to help and protect. In a similar manner, "Minority Units" like the ones established by the Israel National Police, despite what might have been the original impetus behind their creation solidified even further the "otherness" of the Muslim communities and other minority groups.

What Is the Answer Then?

The answer is much more complex than this book allows us to ponder. It is rooted in years of prejudice, bias, and stereotypes that cannot be eliminated within one generation. Yet, there are certain models of policing and movements towards solutions that should serve as a prototype for other police forces that appear to struggle with the notion of equity and parity.

In the year 2010 the Israel National Police employed only less than 2% of the Israeli Arabs (*Jerusalem Post* 2010) yet, in the January 2012, it was announced that the INP plans to recruit hundreds of minorities, over 1,500, and predominantly Israeli Arabs in an initiative to better integrate the minority population in the responsibilities that other Israeli citizens bear (Haaretz 2012). If this initiative indeed sees light of the day, then the minority population, predominantly the minority Muslim population, will constitute about 15% of the INP total sworn staff, which in turn will be much closer to the total number of Muslim minorities in Israel.

This approach, again if implemented, will mirror the approach of the Northern Ireland Police Services and their 50:50 initiative which, so far, appears to be a step in the right direction of integrating various religious backgrounds into mainstream policing in order to create a perception that equity and parity in policing, as far as religious representation is concerned, is up to par with the actual representation of the given religion in the larger population of the country.

The question though remains if such an approach will indeed go beyond numerical representation and will influence police practices perceived by minorities as unjust and discriminatory. The paucity of research existing in this area points to the concept of "double marginality" experienced by the African American population police by the African American police officers. The claims were rather startling when African Americans accused the African American police officers of selling them to the Whites, as part of the assimilation process to the group think of the dominant group. Years after the first empirical research was conducted in this area the minority community rejects the race of police officers involved in excessive or what is perceived as excessive use of force incidents, as an explanation that race was not the factor behind the perceived misconduct. To the contrary, the new concept of Black officers becoming "Blue" (for the color of the police uniform that most of the police forces in the United States wear), took a life of its own, with various advocates of the idea pointing to the fact that the race of the officer has actually nothing to do with the discrimination of the given minority group, claiming that racism is so pervasive in American policing that it trumps the race of the officer (Bolton and Feagin 2004; Roberg et al. 2005; Sullivan, 1989).

Berg et al. (1984), found that Black police officers were less detached and less alienated from the community than officers of other races or ethnic background, but on the other hand they also made a supposition that the Black officers tried to identify with their White colleagues, which basically renders the findings of this research of limited value for a more permanent solution to the effectiveness of diverse force.

On the more encouraging side Weitzer (2000) found that racially mixed policing teams can socialize each other to interact better with the members of the given minorities, in addition to the symbolic value for the communities policed by its members. Overall, however, Roberg et al. (2005) found that the research in this area is too scarce to make any conclusive statements.

Following the aforementioned arguments and the scarcity of the empirical findings one needs to rethink the benefits of recruiting by religion, as it might very well generate the same reaction of the minority population based on the argument that Islamophobia trumps the religion of the Muslim police officer.

The answer then is, maybe, not necessarily just the proportionate recruitment of police officers based on their religious affiliations but rather the concept introduced over a decade ago and referred to as the "triangle of police integrity" (Haberfeld 2012) may provide an answer. The triangle of police integrity refers to the idea of creating and maintaining ethical environments within police organizations that is based on the three prongs of the triangle: recruitment, selection, and training.

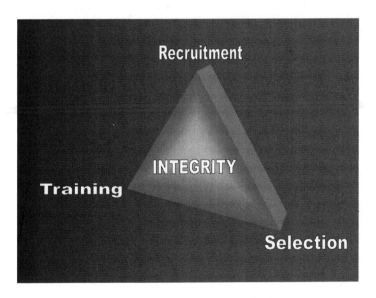

This concept advances the importance of the three components of recruitment, selection, and training as the fundamental building block for police with equity and parity. Casting the net as widely as possible and into as many diverse environments as possible, while looking for the potential recruit, is the first step in assuring equal representation of the community in the policing effort of any given environment.

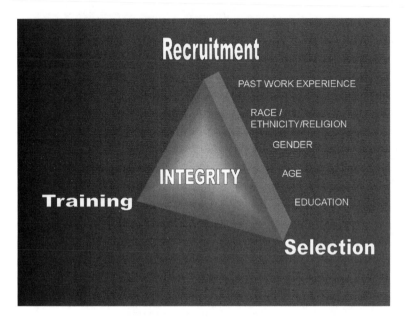

Assuring that factors like past work experience, education, age, gender, race, ethnicity, religion, sexual orientation and more, are all equally targeted allows any police organization to select the most adequate pool of candidates. However this is where the hard work begins, with properly designed and implemented training but without the adequate pool of candidates the dream of professional policing, one based on considerations that are devoid of personal and/or organizational biases, will still remain a mere phantom.

The process of selection, however, is a very complex one, which also more frequently than not involves a number of very problematic considerations that are in nature either politically, professionally, or availability driven. What is meant here by political consideration is the theme or the flavor that any given politician or politicians running for an office want to endorse, based on what the local or state community seems to be asking for at any given point of time.

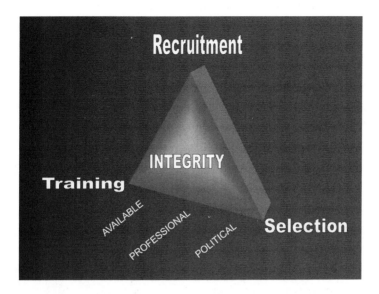

In addition, no matter how wide the agency recruitment net is, the availability of the candidates that can truly fall within the "professional" category is not always there. For example, as previously noted, the Israel National Police plans to recruit over 1,500 minority officers, however, it remains to be seen if these targeted 1,500 are indeed available and if they are do they represent primarily a certain religious background that the INP aims to recruit or do they fall with the "professional" category. Therefore what is this "professional" category? Despite decades of empirical research in the field of policing it is still hard to identify the core requisites for the ideal officer that will satisfy the label of police professionalism. Many agencies around the world stress the importance of education, lack of criminal background, and physical and psychological fitness, yet policing is a very complex profession that certainly requires more than the rather generic set of qualifications. Especially when officers of a given force are required to police ethnic/racial/religious groups, this set of generic qualifiers is rarely a fully sufficient fit.

The last prong of the triangle of police integrity thus must rely on proper training. If an agency cannot cast a wide enough net during the recruitment process or the net is wide enough but does not generate enough candidates for selection and when the selection process is influenced and tainted by various politically and availability related factors, training is the last hope for creating an officer who will adhere to the principles of equity and parity despite personal, societal, and organizational pressure.

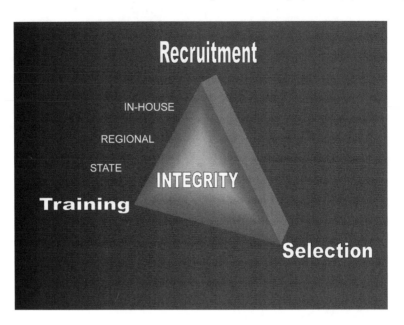

    In the United States police officers can be exposed to one of the three basic types
of training which take place, based on the local jurisdiction, in either in-house,
regional, or state police academies. In other countries around the world the situation
is very similar and depends on the level of centralization or decentralization of a
given police force. The more decentralized the police force is the harder it is to
address, in a truly comprehensive manner, the issues of equity and parity. The more
centralized the force and its training unit is, the more opportunities and therefore
more promise there is to address these so profoundly important concepts/issues in a
way that will truly indoctrinate the recruits and enable them to see beyond the prejudice, stereotype, and moral panic.
    Haberfeld (2002) identified the concept of multicultural close contact training,
one in which members of various ethnic/racial/religious groups are brought together
during the basic academy and assigned group tasks in an attempt to break the preconceived notions and create pathways towards equity and parity in policing, predicated
upon a professional, cohesive team-based approach to problem solving, free of biases
and prejudice. Despite the fact that the concept is over a decade old, its implementation during the basic academy training does not seem to be a part of any of the mandated basic academy training modules, which leads these authors to conclude that the
contours towards equity and parity in policing of various minority groups, and
Muslim communities among them, are already delineated. What is missing is the
willingness of police forces around the world to follow the pathways.

References

Berg, B., True, E., & Gertz, M. (1984). Police, riots, and alienation. *Journal of Police Science and Administration, 12*, 186–190.

Bolton, K., & Feagin, J. R. (2004). *Black in blue: African-American police officers and racism.* New York: Routledge.

Cerrah, I. (2012). Field notes.

Haaretz.com (2012) Retrieved from www.haaretz.com/print-edition/news/israel-plans-to-recruit-hundreds-of-new-arab-police-officers-1.1974, 14 Feb 2012.

Haberfeld, M. R. (2002). *Critical issues in police training.* Upper Saddle River: Prentice Hall.

Haberfeld, M. R. (2012). *Police Leadership: Organizational and managerial decision making process* (2nd ed.). Upper Saddle River: Pearson Custom Publishing.

Jerusalem Post (2010) Retrieved from http://www.jpost.com/Israel/Article.aspx?id=169697, 14 Feb 2012.

Roberg, R., Novak, K., & Cordner, G. (2005). *Police and society* (3rd ed.). Los Angeles: Roxbury Publishing Company.

Sullivan, P. S. (1989). Minority officers: Current issues. In R. G. Dunham & G. P. Alpert (Eds.), *Critical issues in policing: Contemporary readings* (pp. 311–345). Prospect Heights: Waveland.

Weitzer, R. (2000). White, black, or blue cops? Race and citizen assessment of police officers. *Journal of Criminal Justice, 28*, 313–324.

Index

F.B. Hakeem et al., *Policing Muslim Communities: Comparative International Context*,   141
DOI 10.1007/978-1-4614-3552-5, © Springer Science+Business Media New York 2012